New Directions for
Adult and Continuing
Education

D1614284

Jovita M. Ross-Gordon
Joellen E. Coryell
COEDITORS-IN-CHIEF

Turning Points: Recent Trends in Adult Basic Literacy, Numeracy, and Language Education

Alisa Belzer

EDITOR

Number 155 • Fall 2017
Jossey-Bass
San Francisco

Turning Points: Recent Trends in Adult Basic Literacy, Numeracy, and Language Education
Alisa Belzer (ed.)
New Directions for Adult and Continuing Education, no. 155
Coeditors-in-Chief: *Jovita M. Ross-Gordon and Joellen E. Coryell*

NEW DIRECTIONS FOR ADULT AND CONTINUING EDUCATION, (Print ISSN: 1052-2891; Online ISSN: 1536-0717), is published quarterly by Wiley Subscription Services, Inc., a Wiley Company, 111 River St., Hoboken, NJ 07030-5774 USA.

Postmaster: Send all address changes to NEW DIRECTIONS FOR ADULT AND CONTINUING EDUCATION, John Wiley & Sons Inc., C/O The Sheridan Press, PO Box 465, Hanover, PA 17331 USA.

Copyright and Copying (in any format)

Information for subscribers

NEW DIRECTIONS FOR ADULT AND CONTINUING EDUCATION is published in 4 issues per year. Institutional subscription prices for 2017 are:

Print & Online: US$454 (US), US$507 (Canada & Mexico), US$554 (Rest of World), €363 (Europe), £285 (UK). Prices are exclusive of tax. Asia-Pacific GST, Canadian GST/HST and European VAT will be applied at the appropriate rates. For more information on current tax rates, please go to www.wileyonlinelibrary.com/tax-vat. The price includes online access to the current and all online back-files to January 1st 2013, where available. For other pricing options, including access information and terms and conditions, please visit www.wileyonlinelibrary.com/access.

Delivery Terms and Legal Title

Where the subscription price includes print issues and delivery is to the recipient's address, delivery terms are **Delivered at Place (DAP)**; the recipient is responsible for paying any import duty or taxes. Title to all issues transfers FOB our shipping point, freight prepaid. We will endeavour to fulfil claims for missing or damaged copies within six months of publication, within our reasonable discretion and subject to availability.

Back issues: Single issues from current and recent volumes are available at the current single issue price from cs-journals@wiley.com.

Disclaimer

The Publisher and Editors cannot be held responsible for errors or any consequences arising from the use of information contained in this journal; the views and opinions expressed do not necessarily reflect those of the Publisher and Editors, neither does the publication of advertisements constitute any endorsement by the Publisher and Editors of the products advertised.

Publisher: NEW DIRECTIONS FOR ADULT AND CONTINUING EDUCATION is published by Wiley Periodicals, Inc., 350 Main St., Malden, MA 02148-5020.

Journal Customer Services: For ordering information, claims and any enquiry concerning your journal subscription please go to www.wileycustomerhelp.com/ask or contact your nearest office.
Americas: Email: cs-journals@wiley.com; Tel: +1 781 388 8598 or +1 800 835 6770 (toll free in the USA & Canada).
Europe, Middle East and Africa: Email: cs-journals@wiley.com; Tel: +44 (0) 1865 778315.
Asia Pacific: Email: cs-journals@wiley.com; Tel: +65 6511 8000.
Japan: For Japanese speaking support, Email: cs-japan@wiley.com.
Visit our Online Customer Help available in 7 languages at www.wileycustomerhelp.com/ask

Production Editor: Abha Mehta (email: abmehta@wiley.com).

Wiley's Corporate Citizenship initiative seeks to address the environmental, social, economic, and ethical challenges faced in our business and which are important to our diverse stakeholder groups. Since launching the initiative, we have focused on sharing our content with those in need, enhancing community philanthropy, reducing our carbon impact, creating global guidelines and best practices for paper use, establishing a vendor code of ethics, and engaging our colleagues and other stakeholders in our efforts. Follow our progress at www.wiley.com/go/citizenship

View this journal online at wileyonlinelibrary.com/journal/ace

Wiley is a founding member of the UN-backed HINARI, AGORA, and OARE initiatives. They are now collectively known as Research4Life, making online scientific content available free or at nominal cost to researchers in developing countries. Please visit Wiley's Content Access - Corporate Citizenship site: http://www.wiley.com/WileyCDA/Section/id-390082.html

Printed in the USA by The Sheridan Group.

Address for Editorial Correspondence: Coeditors-in-Chief, *Jovita M. Ross-Gordon and Joellen E. Coryell, NEW DIRECTIONS FOR ADULT AND CONTINUING EDUCATION,* Email: jross-gordon@txstate.edu

Abstracting and Indexing Services

The Journal is indexed by Academic Search Alumni Edition (EBSCO Publishing); ERIC: Educational Resources Information Center (CSC); Higher Education Abstracts (Claremont Graduate University); Sociological Abstracts (ProQuest).

Cover design: Wiley
Cover Images: © Lava 4 images | Shutterstock

For submission instructions, subscription and all other information visit:
wileyonlinelibrary.com/journal/ace

CONTENTS

EDITOR'S NOTES

The Program for International Assessment of Adult Competencies finds that 36 million adults in the United States struggle to use reading to support and enhance their day-to-day activities (Organisation for Economic Cooperation and Development, 2013). Increased literacy levels are linked to improved personal outcomes with regard to individual earnings and employment status; improved educational outcomes for children; and health and socioeconomic outcomes in terms of productivity, a strengthened economy based on higher wages, and a more engaged civic and community citizenry (U.S. Department of Education, Office of Career, Technical, and Adult Education, 2015). The need for adult basic education (ABE) is clear. Yet, ABE, which includes basic literacy, numeracy, and language education as well as high school equivalency preparation, is an educational arena that seems to be in constant need of further development, struggles for funding, and lacks a solid research base.

Although ABE has been federally funded since 1964, the National Literacy Act, the funding authorization for ABE that passed in 1991, engendered much needed infrastructure development for the field. The Workforce Investment Act (WIA) of 1998, the next federal authorization, gave rise to a fully developed accountability system. All else aside, these changes had major impacts on the field. However, in the nearly 20 years since WIA was enacted, the field had been more or less static because there were no major policy initiatives. This all began to change around 2014 when a new version of the General Educational Development (GED) test was launched, new content standards were developed, new data on adult cognitive skills were released, and a long delayed new federal adult education authorization, known as the Workforce Innovation and Opportunity Act (WIOA) with its emphasis (almost to the exclusion of all else) on employment and training was enacted. This was certainly a turning point. A few years later, it now seems an appropriate time to review where the field is now in relationship to where it has been and where it could go. This volume was conceptualized to accomplish this by taking up critical discussions of these major changes as well as topics of enduring interest.

In Chapter 1, I give an overview of the policy history and point out how it has created infrastructure and institutionalization, helping to make the field more stable. However, I note that as more systems and structures have been put in place, ABE is in danger of narrowing rather than focusing. I identify focus as being the impetus for the development of rich resources and instructional strategies that help practitioners respond effectively to learner needs, interests, and goals. In contrast, narrowing can limit its efforts to very few goals and give value to only some outcomes. Although the former can be learner centered, the latter is driven more by policy ideals that may or may not align with learners' purposes for participating in ABE.

New Directions for Adult and Continuing Education, no. 155, Fall 2017 © 2017 Wiley Periodicals, Inc.
Published online in Wiley Online Library (wileyonlinelibrary.com) • DOI: 10.1002/ace.20235

In Chapter 2, Jacobson describes WIOA, contrasts it with earlier federal funding legislation, and problematizes its potential impact. He contextualizes his description in long-standing challenges that the field has faced. These include debates about the purposes of adult education; marginalization of adult education, which contributes to inadequate and unstable funding; and the tendency to try to hold programs accountable for outcomes only some of which they have control over. These challenges can be understood as an overestimation of and perhaps unrealistic optimism about what practitioners and learners can accomplish under the circumstances. WIOA makes clear that, in spite of ongoing debates in this area, the policy purpose of adult education is leaning ever more toward it being primarily in service of employment goals and economic competitiveness on a macro scale. Thus, policymakers are assuming that practitioners can help learners overcome multiple barriers to employment that many low-skilled job seekers experience. Thus, they are often trying to help learners meet funders' and their own goals for employment in addition to helping them address other diverse needs and broad goals. By drastically underfunding the system, as Jacobson illustrates, they are also assuming that practitioners can accomplish a mighty task with inadequate resources.

In stark contrast to the narrowing focus on employment that many read into WIOA, Chapter 3 describes the frameworks that guided the development of the Organisation for Economic Cooperation and Development's (OECD) Program for the International Assessment of Adult Competence (PIAAC) in three domains: literacy, numeracy, and problem solving in a technology-rich environment. These frameworks were developed in light of OECD efforts to define what it means to be competent in adulthood. Three broad categories of competence were identified: autonomy, tools use, and social interaction; the notion of competence was inextricably tied to skill use in daily life, including but not exclusively in work settings. Stein points out that the definitional frameworks that guided PIAAC development can also be used to strengthen instruction in ways that focus on the context, content, and cognitive strategies that shape literacy and numeracy practices in adults' day-to-day interactions. Although a broader conception of the purposes for adult education is implied in the PIAAC frameworks (in contrast with WIOA), Stein suggests that teaching to this test may actually make U.S. adults far more competitive with their international counterparts.

Chapter 4 focuses on a turning point that has had a critical impact on practice: changes in high school equivalency testing. The initial change, a revision of the GED® test, was prompted by the adoption of the K–12 Common Core State Standards (CCSS), which established new, rigorous expectations for students. Matching the trend of new standardized tests designed to capture progress toward meeting CCSS standards, the GED® test was updated to reflect Career and College Readiness Standards (CCRS) implemented for adult learners but preserving many of the same intentions of the CCSS. However, pushback and resistance related to many changes surrounding this update "opened the door" (McLendon, Chapter 4) to competition from other test

New Directions for Adult and Continuing Education • DOI: 10.1002/ace

developers. After having a monopoly on high school equivalency testing since its inception, the GED® now faces competition from two other major test developers. Although in many ways the GED® alignment with the rigorous CCRS is more momentous than this recent added market competition, McClendon argues that more players in the arena could lead to better assessment practices.

In Chapter 5, Rosen and Vanek outline the ways in which an explosion of technology and huge leaps forward in access to information and educational opportunities via smartphones and widespread Internet access are changing the ways in which individuals can learn. With an emphasis on learning about technology for a broad range of purposes rather than for its own sake, they suggest that technology can enhance "lifewide" learning. However, benefitting in ABE from all the affordances of technology, they point out, is challenged by the same issues that undermine so much about this field: underfunding, low instructional capacity hindered by limited and often ineffective professional development, and ambiguous policy direction. In order for technology to reach its rich potential in supporting adult learning, practitioners must help learners bridge the digital divide, which is now less about access to tools and more about the development of informed, skilled, and savvy users who can strategically and effectively deploy technology to meet their needs and interests.

Chapter 6 is written in the context of the current immigration wave, the biggest and longest in U.S. history (Population Reference Bureau, n.d.), albeit one that might soon end as a result of ongoing calls for immigration reform and a new administration that has begun to focus inward. Larrotta points out that immigrants are identified as being in one of two categories—documented and undocumented—that are particularly salient to delineating opportunities to participate in adult education. Although integration is key to economic self-sufficiency, and English language learning, civics education, and survival skills particular to life in the United States are of critical importance, only documented immigrants have full access to federally funded adult education, and that access may be limited because of insufficient funding and program availability. She observes that many nonprofit community and church-based organizations have taken up the slack for both documented and undocumented immigrants. Yet they often do so with limited and unstable resources. Larrotta suggests that it is in the nation's best interest to more fully support the immigrant integration effort regardless of how individuals got to the United States.

Professional development and professionalization trends are updated in Chapter 7. In particular, Smith documents the growing institutionalization of professional development for adult basic education practitioners. The main impetus for this has been a WIA regulation that requires states to set aside money for leadership activities including professional development. Perhaps not coincidentally, this same legislation has increased accountability demands and encouraged more rigorous performance standards that in turn led to more rigorous high school equivalency tests. These factors may also have created a much clearer and focused need for professional development in the field.

In the early 2000s, subsequent to WIA enactment, there was growing energy focused on establishing professional development systems at the state level. More recently, the field has moved toward a greater effort to increase professional development quality by drawing on a robust best-practices research base and increasing access to professional resources through online sources along with efforts to professionalize the field through credentialing. It is unclear how mandates for high-quality professional development called for in WIOA will intersect with the priorities of the new administration which could lead to cuts in funding and changing priorities for adult education.

In Chapter 8, Greenberg, Ginsburg, and Wrigley provide helpful overviews of current research in reading, numeracy, and language education. Although WIOA points us toward reading for employment and PIAAC points us toward reading (literacy) for a broad range of uses that contribute to a "successful" life, Greenberg notes that much of the current research on adult literacy has focused on the components that support reading comprehension. Ginsburg reviews the research on transfer of numeracy understanding and skill from the workplace to the classroom and back. She asserts that more research and improved practice are needed to take better advantage of the connections that could be made between them if each context could be understood as a resource to support learning in the other. Wrigley points out that, despite the important returns that can be reaped from increased English proficiency among immigrant adults, the knowledge base on effective practices is especially limited. This problem is exacerbated by the complexity and variety of the target population (immigrants with limited English proficiency) and a severe lack of funding for research and development. Although each section of this chapter is diverse, all could end with the same sentence: "More research is needed to address this complex instructional challenge".

In this volume's concluding chapter, Prins amplifies on this theme by pointing to the many gaps in the research base that this volume illuminates; the ways in which research could strengthen policymaking and practice; and how diverse research approaches that include university researchers, practitioners, and learners can enrich the knowledge base in important ways. This volume is timely in capturing the changing landscape and, it is hoped, will serve as a guidepost to current conditions and challenges for a range of interested stakeholders.

Alisa Belzer
Editor

References

Organisation for Economic Cooperation and Development. (2013). *Time for the U.S. to reskill? What the survey of adult skills says.* Paris: OECD Publishing. https://doi.org/10.1787/9789264204904-en

Population Reference Bureau. (n.d.). *Trends in migration to the U.S.* Retrieved from http://www.prb.org/Publications/Articles/2014/us-migration-trends.aspx
U.S. Department of Education Office of Career, Technical, and Adult Education. (2015). *Making skills everyone's business: A call to transform adult learning in the United States.* Washington, DC: Author.

ALISA BELZER is an associate professor at the Graduate School of Education, Rutgers University. She is program coordinator of the EdM in Adult and Continuing Education at Rutgers and coeditor of the Journal of Research and Practice for Adult Literacy, Secondary, and Basic Education.

This chapter reviews the implications of policy as it has affected adult basic education over the last 25 years and problematizes the increasing institutionalization and stability that it has brought to the field.

Focusing or Narrowing: Trade-Offs in the Development of Adult Basic Education, 1991–2015

Alisa Belzer

Federal money provides less than half of all the funding that supports the provision of adult basic education (ABE) (basic literacy, numeracy, English language, and adult secondary education) in the United States (Foster & McLendon, 2012). Yet, it influences the direction of the field (by which I mean service provision and the practitioners that support it) in substantial ways. The federal government initially used its support of the field primarily to help it grow, develop, and become more stable (Rose, 1991; U.S. Department of Education, Office of Vocational and Adult Education [USDOE OVAE], 2013). In recent years, it has also taken a more active role in standardizing practice, increasing accountability, and seeking to improve the quality of services. It has done this primarily through legislative policy and regulation. By distributing federal funds through a single state agency, which in turn allocates them to local programs, it has been able both to hold states accountable for meeting performance standards and given them the latitude to determine how they will meet them. In this chapter, I trace the ways in which federal policy has served to focus and institutionalize the field in ways that seem to insure its survival but at the same time problematically narrow definitions of ABE—literacy in particular—and the role of adult learners in setting their educational pathway.

Using the metaphors of focusing and narrowing can help frame the path that ABE policy has taken over the last 25 years. Focusing suggests seeing with greater clarity, sharpness, and detail. When applied to ABE, it suggests a rich, complex view of literacy as a diverse set of social practices that vary in application depending on purpose, text, task, and context. Additionally, focus would bring a deeper understanding of the complex, multifaceted, and rich experiences of adult learners that shape their needs, interests, and goals for

New Directions for Adult and Continuing Education, no. 155, Fall 2017 © 2017 Wiley Periodicals, Inc.
Published online in Wiley Online Library (wileyonlinelibrary.com) • DOI: 10.1002/ace.20236

participating in adult education in diverse ways. Focus would support the development of instructional materials, assessment strategies, program accountability, and instruction based on learner-centered approaches. Narrowing indicates a limiting process that requires funders, practitioners, and learners to be selective in conceptions of literacy and the purposes of adult education. It may also tend to limit conceptions of adult learners in terms of their goals for adult education. In turn, this could limit instructional and assessment strategies, what is measured for accountability purposes, and the role of learners in shaping their educational experiences.

Federal funding for ABE has been allocated annually since 1964; over the last 25 years, the statute that authorizes this has been updated just three times. In 1991 the National Literacy Act (NLA) adopted a new, broader, and more humanistic definition of literacy that focused on the day-to-day goals of adults and the uses of literacy as they defined them. The Workforce Investment Act (WIA), approved in 1998, initiated a national accountability system that was tied to federal funding and reaffirmed and strengthened the connection between basic skills and work. Soon after the NLA and WIA were passed, major summaries of the "state of the field" were published (Belzer & St. Clair, 2003; Fingeret, 1992) that sought to capture what made the new legislation distinctive and how it could potentially (re)shape the field. Similarly, this volume is written at a turning point shaped largely by the passage of the Workforce Innovation and Opportunity Act (WIOA) of 2014. This chapter summarizes these prior publications and raises questions about and problematizes the current state of the field in terms of focusing and narrowing.

The National Literacy Act: Institutionalizing the Adult Literacy Infrastructure

Fingeret (1992) wrote an overview of and vision for the field soon after the NLA was enacted. She argued that, prior to the NLA, the federal approach to ABE funding had been to treat low literacy among adults as a short-term crisis that could be quickly addressed and eliminated. This played out in limited infrastructure development in the field. However, several elements of the NLA seemed to signal a more long-term commitment to improving ABE and acknowledge it as an ongoing need. To that end, the NLA began to construct a more permanent infrastructure. Important indicators of this change were the establishment of the National Institute for Literacy (NIFL), State Literacy Resource Centers (SLRCs), and the requirement that states develop indicators of program quality along with performance standards that would enable the state agency responsible for funding ABE to evaluate local program needs for technical assistance and make more informed funding decisions. There was also a specific focus on workforce development through the National Workforce Demonstration Projects and family literacy through an expansion of Evenstart to include adult education as a required element of the program (USDOE OVAE, 2013). For the first time, adult basic education was framed not so much as a strategy for reducing poverty but rather as an important element in strengthening the economy and increasing U.S. competitiveness as major trends in globalization were emerging (Sticht, 2002). Yet, it was also a time when learner experiences, perspectives, and goals were increasingly valued for the ways they could and should inform instruction and program management.

As a result, Fingeret observed (and advocated for) an increased interest in learner-centered and participatory instructional and program models. Along with this, qualitative and holistic methods for assessing learning were developing. These focused on understanding changes in learners' literacy practices in a range of contexts, the literacy strategies they deployed to make meaning from a variety of texts, and progress in meeting self-identified goals. Grounded in a sociocultural perspective on literacy (Street, 1984), practitioners worked to develop strategies to document learning growth in ways that captured this kind of progress. Similarly, program evaluation that described processes and values as well as accomplishments in helping students meet their goals was understood to be of value (Lytle & Wolfe, 1989). Although on the one hand, requirements for indicators of program quality and increased coordination across the education, training, and employer sectors could increase standardization and potentially narrow the field, efforts to value learner perspectives, experiences, cultures, and goals could help maintain diversity in the field (Beder, 1991).

Although the NLA seemed to increase infrastructure for the field, Fingeret identified several areas of ongoing need, especially in the area of professional development. She argued that professional development should help practitioners strengthen their ability to take a critical perspective and an inquiry stance on their practice and that it should be ongoing, embedded, and teacher driven. There were also gaps in curricular resources. For example, although the roots of an integrated job training and education system were present in the NLA and would later be mandated in WIA and strengthened in the WIOA, she noted that, at the time, "the majority of materials relating to work and education remain based in theory more than in experience and practice" (p. 35).

In spite of an ongoing ideological connection between adult literacy education, poverty reduction, and employment and economic development that was present in the NLA, the 1990s as foretold by Fingeret's monograph, written in the early part of the decade, was also a time of burgeoning learner leadership, valuing of learner voice, and at least for some, dedication to literacy education as social justice. She identified this era as one in which understandings of literacy as a neutral, unchanging set of skills shifted to conceptions of literacy as a meaning-based and contextualized social practice that varies by purpose, task, and audience. Fingeret also described it as a time when literacy education was understood as contributing to equity and social justice, and "a political statement about the dignity and rights of every human being" (p. 45). This era seemed to support increased focus.

The Workforce Investment Act: Coordination and Accountability

With the WIA, ABE was subsumed within the workforce development system in 1998. Although a separate title of the law, it was now mandated to join with the employment and training sectors in an effort to increase coordination, reduce redundancies, and increase accountability (Belzer & St. Clair, 2003; USDOE OVAE, 2013). Given that many users of the employment, training, and adult education systems participate in services offered in more than one of these sectors, coordination and joint planning among them can be understood as a logical efficiency. Partnerships were enacted through Workforce Investment Boards and "one-stop" centers that had the goal of meeting multiple service needs for clients through colocation. The impetus for mandated coordination across the training, employment, and education sectors was the assumption that the success of the economy is tied to the success of the education and training system for youth and adults (USDOE OVAE, 2013).

In addition to the very significant and explicit shift from education to employment as a key driving force for practice, perhaps the most consequential change for day-to-day program management and instruction was the institution of a national performance accountability system. The National Reporting System (NRS) was implemented to evaluate effectiveness and encourage ongoing program improvement, and it influenced instruction and program management in substantive ways (Belzer, 2007). It required states to aggregate local program data on five core measures: educational gains (as measured by standardized tests), attainment of a high school diploma, entrance into postsecondary education or training, and obtaining or retaining a job. Extensive training at the state and federal levels was implemented to build understanding of the accountability system and support development of an infrastructure around assessment and data management. The goal was that programs could accurately report outcomes data to the state agency responsible for managing federal adult education funds, which would in turn report to the federal government. In addition to the strong influence of WIA, the "work first" philosophy forwarded by welfare reform legislation enacted in 1998 contributed to the movement in many programs to shift their emphasis to job search and retention skills and to otherwise limit instruction to skill development that could be measured by standardized tests. This was further reinforced by a growing expectation that practice should be "evidence-based" despite a very limited knowledge base (Kruidenier, 2002).

In an overview of the field composed five years after WIA was enacted, Belzer and St. Clair (2003) saw the increasing institutionalization of the field that was supported and encouraged through implementation of WIA as both an opportunity and a limitation whose consequences had yet to fully play out. We observed, however, that Fingeret's optimism in the 1990s was not fully realized. In particular, the expectation that learners could shape their learning and influence program management and the concept that rich information drawn from formative, qualitative assessments that focus on adults' uses of reading and writing in their day-to-day lives should shape instruction were not realized in the new accountability climate. Instead, programs that had emphasized adult literacy education for personal development, empowerment, and student-identified goals found themselves narrowing their mission to more measurable, concrete outcomes (Belzer, 2007). It could be argued that the field was, in part, a victim of its success. As its visibility rose, it was more influenced by broader trends in education, especially with regard to accountability.

The challenge, as we posed it in that paper, was maintaining a focus on both learner goals and accountability demands when these do not necessarily obviously overlap. We argued that the structures and expectations put in place by WIA could be understood as providing additional, needed structure and focus when it draws on effective practices and learner needs. However, when systems are put in place for bureaucratic, political, or ideological reasons, they can be counterproductive and narrowing. When we wrote the paper, it was not entirely clear what the long-term impact of WIA would be. Research conducted after a few years of WIA implementation did document impact on program structures, formats, and procedures (Belzer, 2007), but there has been no research on how this policy shift affected learner outcomes. This gap is not easily filled; like much accountability data, the data that have been collected for the NRS are not designed for or particularly useful for most research purposes (Hamilton, 2003). Although methods for using assessment data to improve practice are understood (e.g., Earl, 2012), the way in which they may actually affect practice and policy is problematic (Hamilton & Barton, 2000). At any rate, a lack of rigorous research about the relationship between various interventions, initiatives, quality improvement efforts, and a range of learner outcomes leave our ability to make judgments about the impact of WIA elusive.

The Workforce Opportunity and Innovation Act: Education as an Employment Activity

WIA was due to expire in 2003 but was not replaced until 2014 with the Workforce Opportunity and Innovation Act. In many ways, WIOA is a strengthening of principles established in WIA, especially related to efficiency and cooperation among the employment, training, and adult education sectors with the primary goal of increasing employment opportunities for participants. For the first time, common performance indicators and a single state plan are required across all six core programs in employment, training, and adult education. By requiring an integrated approach to education and training, WIOA further establishes adult education as essentially in support of federal employment goals. This signals a shift away from conceptions of adult education as helping learners more effectively fulfill a range of roles in addition to that of worker. A broader conception had been codified in the content standards, Equipped for the Future, which were developed by NIFL in the 1990s and subsequently adopted by many state adult education agencies and local programs. Instead, according to an informational document distributed by the U.S. Department of Education (2014), "WIOA recognizes that the core purpose of adult education is to prepare individuals with the skills and knowledge needed to succeed in postsecondary education and the workforce" (p. 2). This is operationalized by various integrated training and education models and so-called career pathways as well as recently developed career and college readiness standards. WIOA is described in greater detail by Jacobson (Chapter 2, this volume).

Trade-Offs for the Field

This brief history of recent statutes and interpretation of those statutes describes a relatively young educational system that has shown clear signs of maturation and development over the last 25 years. Yet, with its robust integration with the employment and training sectors mandated by WIOA, it leans toward framing adult learners primarily as employees or potential employees whose primary educational task is to fulfill labor demands and contribute to the economic competitiveness of our country on the global stage. Although definitions of literacy have continued to broaden, becoming richer and more complex in some arenas (Belzer, in press; Stein, this volume), WIOA seems to imply a conception of literacy that has narrowed to a specific set of tasks and purposes related to employment. Similarly, learners are assumed to have employment as their primary goal (postsecondary education, although a key goal of WIOA, is framed primarily as a step along the way to employment and increased earnings) and have thus largely been removed from discussions about their goals for learning, their purposes for literacy, and how they could inform policy, practice, and research.

Long-term, stable funding, and a well-trained workforce are the hope for the field and for the learners it serves. Although funding remains less than adequate and could be further threatened by the priorities of the new administration, commitment to adult education seems stable after more than 50 years of continuous funding. However, that commitment comes with strings attached in that ABE must now be tied in to the employment and training system, and success must be measured around a fairly narrow set of criteria. Employment and the potential to earn a family-sustaining wage are certainly important goals to many adult learners, but adults fulfill many other roles, in addition to worker, that could be supported by increased literacy skill. Focusing is helpful for the field as it can support clear articulation of aims, curriculum development, and professional development that can contribute to a range of learner outcomes; it is especially important in providing a richer, clearer picture of learners, literacy, and adult basic education. On the other hand, narrowing limits the potential of adult education to support literacy, numeracy, and language development across a range of tasks and texts as adults carry out their roles not only as workers but as family members, community members, and citizens. However, as the field has developed, it has tended toward narrowing; researchers, practitioners, and policymakers should instead seek focusing. In this way, adult basic education could meet a broad range of needs, purposes, and goals that would not only respond to diverse adult learners but would also enrich communities, workplaces, and the civic life of our country.

References

Beder, H. (1991). *Adult literacy: Issues for policy and practice.* Malabar, FL: Krieger.

Belzer, A. (2007). Implementing the Workforce Investment Act from in-between: State agency responses to federal accountability policy in adult basic education. *Educational Policy, 21*(4), 555–588.

Belzer, A. (in press). Reflections on the PIAAC literacy and numeracy frameworks and a system that is designed to achieve the results it gets. *Adult Learning.*

Belzer, A., & St. Clair, R. (2003). *Opportunities and limits: An update on adult literacy education.* Columbus, OH: Ohio State University, ERIC Clearinghouse on Adult, Career, and Vocational education.

Earl, L. M. (2012). *Assessment as learning: Using classroom assessment to maximize student learning.* Thousand Oaks, CA: Corwin Press.

Fingeret, A. (1992). *Adult literacy education: Current and future directions. An update.* Columbus, OH: Ohio State University, ERIC Clearinghouse on Adult, Career, and Vocational Education (ED 354 391).

Foster, M., & McLendon, L. (2012). *Sinking or swimming: Findings from a survey of state adult education and financing policies.* Washington, DC: CLASP and National Council of State Directors of Adult Education.

Hamilton, L. (2003). Chapter 2: Assessment as a policy tool. *Review of Research in Education, 27*(1), 25–68.

Hamilton, M., & Barton, D. (2000). The international adult literacy survey: What does it really measure? *International Review of Education, 46*(5), 377–389.

Kruidenier, J. (2002). *Research-based principles for adult basic education reading instruction.* Portsmouth, NH: RMC Corporation.

Lytle, S., & Wolfe, M. (1989). *Adult literacy education: Program evaluation and learner assessment.* Columbus, OH: Ohio State University, ERIC Clearinghouse on Adult, Career, and Vocational Education.

Rose, A. D. (1991). *Ends or means: An overview of the history of the adult education act (Information Series No. 346).* Columbus, OH: Ohio State University, ERIC Clearinghouse on Adult, Career, and Vocational Education.

Sticht, T. G. (2002). The rise of the adult education and literacy system in the United States: 1600–2000. In J. Coming, B. Garner, & C. Smith (Eds.), *The annual review of adult learning and literacy* (pp. 12–43). San Francisco: Jossey-Bass.

Street, B. (1984). *Literacy in theory and practice.* London: Cambridge University Press.

U.S. Department of Education, Office of Vocational and Adult Education. (2013). *An American heritage—Federal adult education: A legislative history 1964–2013.* Washington, DC: Author.

U.S. Department of Education. (2014). The Workforce Innovation and Opportunity Act Overview of Title II: Adult education and literacy. Retrieved from https://www2.ed.gov/about/offices/list/ovae/pi/AdultEd/wioa-overview.pdf

ALISA BELZER is an associate professor at the Graduate School of Education, Rutgers University. She is program coordinator of the EdM in Adult and Continuing Education at Rutgers and coeditor of the Journal of Research and Practice for Adult Literacy Secondary, and Basic Education.

New Directions for Adult and Continuing Education • DOI: 10.1002/ace

2

This chapter reviews how the impact of WIOA on adult education provision in the United States may be limited because of persistent structural problems within adult education policy and practice.

The Workforce Investment and Opportunity Act: New Policy Developments and Persistent Issues

Erik Jacobson

When the Workforce Investment and Opportunity Act (WIOA) was passed by the United States Congress in 2014, it reauthorized federal funding for adult basic education (ABE), which includes workforce training and English for speakers of other languages (ESOL), adult literacy, and high school equivalency programs. Prior to the passage of this legislation, federal support for ABE was authorized by the Workforce Investment Act (WIA), which had not been reauthorized since it was signed into law in 1998 (although it continued to be funded). For this reason, a key promise of WIOA was to update provision of services to meet the needs of a changing economy and workforce. Passage of WIOA was celebrated by some adult education advocates as a sign that more attention was now being paid to the needs of both the workforce and adults in need of basic education (Bird, Foster, & Ganzglass, 2014). Others were concerned that WIOA could actually reduce access to educational services for some learners (e.g., Migration Policy Institute, 2015). This chapter reviews key aspects of WIOA that distinguish it from WIA, the implementation challenges it presents, and what continuities in federal policy suggest about persistent structural issues within adult education provision in the United States.

Federal Adult Education Legislation in the United States

As with public education more generally, the level and type of federal support for adult education in the United States are shaped by the dynamics of particular political moments. For example, in 1964, when the federal government funded adult education through Title IIB of the Economic Opportunity Act, support for education was one part of the larger "War on Poverty." Adult education had become part of the act only after years of advocacy and policy work

New Directions for Adult and Continuing Education, no. 155, Fall 2017 © 2017 Wiley Periodicals, Inc.
Published online in Wiley Online Library (wileyonlinelibrary.com) • DOI: 10.1002/ace.20237

by groups with sometimes contrasting visions for what adult education could and should be (see Rose, 1991, and Sticht, 2002, for detailed accounts). In the end, support for adult education was framed mainly in economic terms, conceived as a means of moving people out of poverty rather than as securing individuals' rights to education (Rose, 1991, p. 16). In 1966, Title IIB was reauthorized as the Adult Education Act.

The National Literacy Act of 1991 amended the Adult Education Act. The use of the word "literacy" in the title is noteworthy. This indicated that rather than being framed in purely economic terms, the act was presented as consistent with the larger federal goal of helping make every adult literate by the year 2000 (Irwin, 1991, p. 7). The act nearly doubled the budget for literacy programs (from $276.5 million to $482.5 million). It created the National Institute for Literacy, which was directed to support basic and applied research on adult literacy (Irwin, 1991, p. 4). The act also funded a grant program for state literacy resource centers, in part, to better coordinate literacy services provision and to promote "state-of-the-art teaching methods" (Irwin, 1991, p. 12).

In 1998, Title II was reauthorized as part of the Workforce Investment Act (WIA) and was renamed the Adult Education and Family Literacy Act (AEFLA). Once again a key goal of the act was to better coordinate adult education services and to establish links between literacy and workforce training programs. WIA placed a strong emphasis on moving adults into employment. This was consistent with the political dynamic of the time and a logical extension of President Clinton's welfare reform efforts. The Personal Responsibility and Work Opportunity Act's "welfare to work" policies sharply reduced the amount of support that individuals could receive (Imel, 2000) and put new limitations on educational activities for welfare recipients. Notably, WIA mandated participation in the National Reporting System (NRS), which requires that states measure and report on their performance using a common set of metrics (e.g., entry into postsecondary education, obtaining employment). The act also prioritized a pedagogical focus on contextualized education, phonemic awareness, systematic phonics, fluency, and reading comprehension (consistent with contemporary shifts in thinking about reading instruction in K–12).

What Is Different in WIOA?

As with previous iterations of federal policy governing provision of adult education services, WIOA's development was shaped by how lawmakers conceptualize the value of adult education and the role of government. According to an informational document crafted by the U.S. Departments of Education and Labor (2016), "The 21st century public workforce development system created through WIOA builds closer ties between business leaders, State and Local Workforce Development Boards, labor unions, community colleges, nonprofit organizations, youth-serving organizations, and State and Local officials

New Directions for Adult and Continuing Education • DOI: 10.1002/ace

to deliver a more job-driven approach to training and skills development" (p. 1). This language generally echoes several previous calls to align the adult education and workforce training systems in order to make them "job driven," but there are some key changes to adult education under WIOA, including a focus on transitions from ABE to postsecondary education, an integrated approach to training and education, and targeted services for vulnerable populations.

A Focus on Transitions. A joint Department of Education/Department of Labor (DOE/DOL) overview document suggests that "WIOA reauthorized AEFLA in a manner that recognizes that completion of high school is not an end in itself but a means to further opportunities and greater economic self-sufficiency" (U.S. DOE & DOL, 2016, p. 4). Indeed, research indicates that the economic benefits of high school equivalency completion (often in the form of the General Educational Development (GED) certificate) are limited unless that credential is used to enroll in postsecondary education or training (Tyler, 2001). However, a U.S. Census report (2012) notes that in 2008–2009,

> While 73 percent of those who received a high school diploma went on to complete at least some postsecondary education, less than half (43 percent) of GED certificate recipients did so. Furthermore, only 5 percent earned a bachelor's degree or higher. In contrast, of high school diploma holders, 33 percent earned this level of education. (p. 13)

Several factors could explain this disparity, including the rising cost of college. However, in seeking an explanation for the struggle of GED certificate holders to successfully transition to college, Bird, Foster, and Ganzglass (2014) turn a critical eye on adult education programs. They suggest that "a historical emphasis on preparation for high school equivalency assessments in the former Title II did not encourage rigorous, intensive programming designed to help students transition to higher levels of education and training" (p. 7). Rather than high school completion, it is explicit in WIOA that helping learners move on to postsecondary education and/or training is a priority and programs are expected to ensure that learners attain the skills they need to make that transition successfully.

An Integrated Approach to Education and Training. WIOA codifies into law that programs can use Title II funds for the basic skills portion of integrated education and training programs (IET). This means that rather than requiring a student to complete educational programming before moving onto workforce training, students can now participate in them concurrently. For example, students can work on their academic skills while receiving training for industry-specific certifications. The goal is to provide education that is contextualized within employment training programs. Early studies (Joyce Foundation, 2013) indicate that this approach holds promise for students, allowing them to move "farther and faster" (Strawn, 2011) than when enrolled in separate education and training programs.

In support of its employment focus, WIOA requires that states establish what are called "career pathways." These enable learners to identify "on-ramps" into a fully integrated system and then move smoothly from one class to the next until they are ready to find employment. The intention is for career pathways to reflect the needs of employers in a specific region so that students will train for occupations in sectors where there are jobs. Theoretically, a student should be able to begin in a literacy class and, over time, proceed all the way to a technical training program, an IET, or college. Because most programs cannot offer the full range of classes necessary for this type of pathway, a focus has been placed on regionalized planning and coordination between adult education and job training entities.

Targeting Vulnerable Populations. The language of WIOA also requires that service providers focus on meeting the education and employment needs of vulnerable populations including veterans, recipients of public assistance, low-income individuals, and those who are "basic-skills deficient" (including those in need of basic literacy or English language classes). Local education programs are also expected to coordinate their activities with other support services (e.g., mental health, child care, transportation), including those that serve adults with disabilities and special needs. Thus, under WIOA, state and local systems are expected to provide a full range of services to marginalized populations with the understanding that learners will not be successful in education or training without them.

Potential Implementation Challenges

In an attempt to create a "21st century workforce system" that prioritizes transitions to employment and college, WIOA has modified some key aspects of existing adult education policy, including increased demands regarding program planning, coordination, and accountability. Given the complex nature of these changes, it is unlikely that the rollout of WIOA will be smooth or consistent from state to state. In fact, the U.S. Government Accountability Office (2016) already notes that implementation has been hampered by limited guidance and resources. There are also concerns related to curriculum development, regional planning, and outcome measurements.

Content Standards Alignment. WIOA guidelines require that states have "challenging academic content standards" for adults (U.S. DOL, 2016, p. 25). In many cases this is being done by adopting the College and Career Readiness Standards (CCRS) developed by the U.S. Department of Education (Pimentel, 2013). These standards are promoted as a blueprint for the kind of "rigorous" programs that will support transition to college and career training. Pimentel asserts that the CCRS are "ambitious" and that the literacy standards "demand robust analytic and reasoning skills and strong oral and written communication skills" (p. 2). However, the standards do not function as a curriculum or specify how to teach students to master the skills identified. As such, it

New Directions for Adult and Continuing Education • DOI: 10.1002/ace

is up to each state to instantiate their vision of the standards and communicate it to students and teachers.

For standards to have their intended effect, teachers need both to be aware of them and understand how they inform curriculum development, instruction, and assessment. However, policy decisions made at the state level about standards are not always disseminated effectively throughout the adult education system, and teachers in programs may remain unaware or unsure about the changes they are expected to enact. For this reason, in addition to articulating challenging academic standards, states will need to build and sustain robust professional development systems to support their implementation in practice. However, as Smith and Gillespie (2007) highlight, there are many structural challenges with regard to providing high-quality, effective professional development, including limited funding, limited opportunities for extended exploration, and an overreliance upon one-shot workshops. Given the current wide variation in the quantity and quality of professional development across the states (Belzer & Darkenwald-DeCola, 2014), the effective adoption and use of new content standards may be problematic.

Local and Regional Decision Making. Under WIOA, local Workforce Development Boards (WDBs) are responsible for the regional planning necessary to align programs and develop and coordinate coherent career pathways. By law, a majority of the board members are required to come from the business sector, with additional representatives coming from a mix of labor, adult education, government, and community-based organizations. Although they previously were expected to act in an advisory capacity, these local boards must now review Title II funding applications from adult education programs in their area before they are submitted to the state.

There are not much data regarding how well WDBs function as a location for adult education planning, but there is reason for concern. A survey conducted by the National Association of Workforce Boards (n.d.) examined board activity across the country, including their regional planning efforts, their outreach activities, and the topics of discussion during board meetings. The results of the survey suggest that adult education was not a priority and rarely a point of discussion. Similarly, a review of the literacy plans of local workforce boards in New Jersey found significant variations in levels of engagement (Jacobson, 2013). Some boards actively worked with adult education providers in order to craft regional literacy plans, whereas others had outdated literacy plans that lay dormant for years. Because these boards have been given the authority to review Title II funding applications, it is essential that they have a good understanding of adult education and the educational needs of the local community. Rather than just allowing for attendance at WDB meetings in a symbolic capacity, consistent input of adult education and community-based representation must be required.

Standard Outcome Measures. The six core programs funded by WIOA (Adult, Dislocated Worker, Youth, Employment Service, Adult Education, and Vocational Rehabilitation) are required to work together under an aligned, unified state plan, and they will all be evaluated using metrics related to employment and earnings subsequent to program participation, enrollment in and completion of secondary or postsecondary education or training, meeting the needs of employers. As with previous iterations of the act, the use of the common metrics may put pressure on programs to engage in "creaming." That is, programs may give enrollment priority to those students who are mostly likely to have outcomes that will fulfill the expectations noted previously. In part, this is built into any accountability system that uses interval type benchmarks. For example, when looking at the "measurable skills gain" metric, a program receives credit for a successful outcome when a student moves up a level on a standardized assessment. A student who is at the lower end of a benchmark interval may make a great deal of progress in a given period but not cross the gain threshold for moving up a level and thus not count as a positive outcome. By comparison, a student who starts at the higher end of an interval may cross into the next level and count as a positive outcome while not making nearly as much overall process. From a program reporting perspective, such students are more attractive.

Although WIOA prioritizes services for adults who are "basic skills deficient" (including English language learners), individuals with disabilities, and those going through reentry after incarceration, students from these populations may have a hard time demonstrating positive outcomes with regard to employment and income. This may lead to increased pressure to work with student populations who can more easily and quickly meet these measures, leaving certain groups of students who are in serious need of services further marginalized. The potential for group-level creaming led the Migration Policy Institute (2015) to conclude that "the prospects for low-educated and LEP immigrants and refugees receiving needed services under WIOA appear gloomy at this time" (p. 4). As Pickard points out (2016), students who are no longer served by WIOA-funded programs will need to look for services elsewhere, typically in the volunteer sector. Given that these programs often have long waiting lists and limited resources for training, they should not be considered an appropriate "safety valve" for a publicly funded system that encourages programs to shed students who may need intensive and long-term services in order to show gains using WIOA accountability metrics.

The use of the job-driven common metrics may also have a profound effect on particular types of programs. For example, under WIOA, English Literacy (EL)/Civics programs can be funded through two different sections of the law, and there are clear differences between the two provisions. In one, EL/Civics provides instruction for literacy, English language acquisition, citizenship, and civic participation. Programs funded by this section may include, but do not require, workforce development activities (Office of Career, Technical and Adult Education (OCTAE), 2016a, p. 3). States are likewise not required to offer these programs. They are required to offer EL/Civics programs under the other section, however, and these programs must integrate with the local workforce development system and focus on workforce preparation.

EL/Civics has thus been given a guaranteed funding stream, but at the cost of taking on new accountability metrics that may not be a good fit for some learners' needs and interests. For example, there are many immigrants who wish to develop their English skills and who may want help becoming citizens but who do not need workforce training. This includes those who are already employed or the elderly who are out of the workforce. It remains to be seen how many states will be in a position to fund two different types of EL/Civics programs, but it is doubtful that many will, leaving many adults without access to valuable resources.

Persistent Issues with Adult Education Policy in the United States

As noted previously, when the Economic Opportunity Act was passed in 1964, there were competing visions of what the federal approach to adult education should be. The division between those valuing liberal educational models and those valuing education for economic development has persisted over the decades. In the current moment, there is concern that the job-driven nature of WIOA will lead to a narrowing of the focus of adult education (Belzer, this volume; Migration Policy Institute, 2015; Pickard, 2016). The fact that this same concern was expressed just after WIA was passed (Imel, 2000) suggests that WIOA can be seen simply as the latest in a series of federal education policies that frame the purpose of schooling in starkly economic terms. We are thus likely to see not only struggles with implementation of WIOA but continued debate around what the goals of adult education can and should be. As ever, public education will remain a key ideological battleground.

In addition to concerns about the marginalization of outcomes long valued among adult educators (e.g., civic participation, social justice), funding for approved job-driven programs is also problematic. As part of an advocacy initiative asking Congress to double WIOA Title II funding, the National Skills Coalition notes that between FY 2010 and FY 2015, federal funding for adult education decreased by 17% in actual dollars (National Skills Coalition, n.d.). A longer term view of funding trends for adult education paints an even starker picture. In 1965, the federal budget for adult education was $18,600,000 and it provided services for approximately 38,000 students (Sticht, 2002, p. 19). This is roughly $489 per student served. In 2016, the Office for Career, Technical and Adult Education requested $581,955,000 to serve an estimated 1,598,756 students (OCTAE, 2016b, p. 29). This is roughly $364 per student served. On the one hand, compared to 1965, the budget is 31 times larger and 42 times more students are now being served. On the other hand, the per student expenditure has dropped dramatically. Using the government's consumer price index (that accounts for fluctuation in the value of the dollar), if the per student expenditure held steady over the decades, it would have been $3,736 in 2016. That means the current per student expenditure is 10% of what it was in 1965. This drastic reduction of per student support has occurred at the same time programs have been tasked with ever increasing expectations for demonstrating positive outcomes in multiple domains. We need to look deeper than the total budget number when gauging policymakers' support for adult education. The low per student expenditure limits the quality, amount, intensity, and type of services programs can provide. It is not enough to simply raise standards and expectations; without drastic increases in funding, WIOA might end up having a limited impact.

Finally, the continued reliance on outcome measurements that prioritize individuals' employment status and earnings is problematic. For example, under WIOA, programs are held accountable for the number of students who find work. However, the chances of finding employment are associated with the number of opportunities present in an area, not just the level of skill of potential workers (Levine, 2013). Programs are also expected to help learners increase their earning power, but wages are heavily influenced by larger macroeconomic forces that are creating more low-wage jobs (Autor, 2010). In this way, adult education programs are being evaluated for delivering outcomes they have little or no control over. Yet, in pitched battles over government expenditures, a failure to meet expectations could place adult basic education funding at risk of being reduced even further. Innovations in WIOA such as support for integrated education and training programs and a focus on successful transitions into postsecondary education are welcome developments. However, questions remain about how well the current act will be able to consistently produce positive outcomes for learners without there being larger changes in the economy.

References

Autor, D. (2010). *The polarization of job opportunities in the U.S. labor market: Implications for employment and earnings.* Washington, DC: Center for American Progress and the Hamilton Project.

Belzer, A., & Darkenwald-DeCola, J. (2014). *A national scan of entry and ongoing professional requirements and professional development offerings for adult education practitioners.* Washington, DC: National Adult Education Professional Development Consortium. Retrieved from http://www.naepdc.org/NAEPDC±Final±Report±on±Professional± Requirements±and±PD±Offerings.pdf

Bird, K., Foster, M., & Ganzglass, E. (2014). *New opportunities to improve economic and career success for low-income youth and adults.* Washington, DC: Center for Law and Social Policy.

Imel, S. (2000). *Welfare to work: Considerations for adult and vocational educational programs.* Columbus, OH: Ohio State University, ERIC Clearinghouse on Adult, Career, and Vocational Education.

Irwin, P. (1991). *National Literacy Act of 1991: Major provisions of P.L. 102–73.* Washington, DC: Congressional Research Service.

Jacobson, E. (2013). *Investing in New Jersey's adult learners.* Trenton, NJ: State Council for Adult Literacy Services.

Joyce Foundation. (2013). *Shifting gears: Building new pathways for low-skilled workers to succeed in the 21st century economy.* Chicago: Author.

Levine, M. (2013). *The skills gap and unemployment in Wisconsin: Separating fact from fiction.* Milwaukee, WI: University of Wisconsin-Milwaukee, Center for Economic Development.

Migration Policy Institute. (2015). *Comments on proposed rules for implementing provisions of the Workforce Innovation and Opportunity Act of 2014*. Washington, DC: Author.
National Association of Workforce Boards (n.d.). *How Workforce Investment Boards are operating*. Retrieved from http://www.nawb.org/nawb/documents/Research/NAWB ComprehensiveWIBReport.pdf
National Skills Coalition. (n.d.). *Congress should invest in adult basic education*. Retrieved from www.nationalskillscoalition.org/resources/publications/file/Why-Congress-should-invest-in-adult-basic-education.pdf
Office of Career, Technical and Adult Education. (2016a). Integrated English Literacy and Civics Education under the Workforce Innovation and Opportunity Act—Frequently asked questions. Program memorandum OCTAE/DAEL 15–7.
Office of Career, Technical and Adult Education. (2016b). *Career, technical and adult education: Fiscal year 2017 budget request*. Washington, DC: Author.
Pickard, A. (2016). WIOA: Implications for low-scoring adult learners. *Journal of Research and Practice for Adult Literacy, Secondary and Basic Education, 5*(2), 50–55.
Pimentel, S. (2013). *College and career readiness standards*. Washington, DC: U.S. Department of Education.
Rose, A. (1991). *Ends or means: An overview of the history of the Adult Education Act*. Columbus, OH: Ohio State University, ERIC Clearinghouse on Adult, Career, and Vocational Education.
Smith, C., & Gillespie, M. (2007). Research on professional development and teacher change: Implications for adult basic education. In J. Comings, B. Garner, & C. Smith (Eds.), *Review of adult learning and literacy* (Vol. 7, pp. 205–244). New York: Routledge.
Sticht, T. (2002). *The rise of the adult education and literacy system in the United States: 1600–2000*. Retrieved from http://ncsall.net/index.html@id=576
Strawn, J. (2011). *Farther, faster: Six promising programs show how career pathway bridges help basic skills students earn credentials that matter*. Washington, DC: Center for Law and Social Policy.
Tyler, J. (2001). *What do we know about the economic benefits of the GED? A synthesis of evidence from recent research*. Cambridge, MA: National Bureau of Economic Research.
U.S. Census Bureau. (2012). *What it's worth: Field of training and economic status in 2009*. Washington, DC: Author.
U.S. Department of Education & U.S. Department of Labor. (2016). The Workforce Innovation and Opportunity Act final rules: A detailed look. Retrieved from https://www.doleta.gov/WIOA/Docs/Final-Rules-A-Detailed-Look-Fact-Sheet.pdf
U.S. Department of Labor. (2016). *Required elements for submission of the Unified or Combined State Plan and Plan Modifications under the Workforce Innovation and Opportunity Act*. Washington, DC: Author.
U.S. Government Accountability Office. (2016). *Workforce Innovation and Opportunity Act: Information on planned changes to state performance reporting and related changes*. Washington, DC: Author.

ERIK JACOBSON is an associate professor in the Early Childhood, Elementary and Literacy Education Department at Montclair State University. He also teaches ESOL in community-based settings and is on the board of the New Jersey Association for Lifelong Learning.

3

This chapter describes how PIAAC's concept of competency-in-use can support literacy policy and practice focused on adult learners' real needs.

PIAAC: Focusing Adult Learning on Building Adult Competence[1]

Sondra Gayle Stein

In the more than 40 years I have worked in adult literacy education as practitioner, program designer, and policymaker, my work has been shaped by a question shared by many colleagues: What is the most effective way to deliver adult literacy education if our goal is not only to build skills but also to make a difference in our students' lives? In the mid-1970s, when I began teaching adults, the U.S. Department of Education had just published the University of Texas's Adult Performance Level (APL) study (Swiss, 1976). Its focus on adult functional competence was highly congruent with the goals of the workplace education program where I was working; it aimed to help workers develop the reading and math skills they needed to be able to meet their own goals as well as to contribute more fully to the workplace. When I moved on, in the early 1980s, to lead a community-based program that prepared women for the world of work, once again, the goals of the program seemed to demand that we ground teaching and learning in the context of our students' lives, building competence not just around a decontextualized set of skills but in using reading, writing, and math skills to accomplish real-world purposes.

I was privileged, in the following decades, to bring what I had learned as a practitioner into the role of policymaker at the state and national levels. The efforts I helped to shape in those decades, from Massachusetts' collaborative Workplace Education Initiative to the National Institute for Literacy's Equipped for the Future Initiative, all built on the assumption that our goal as adult educators was not simply to raise adult learners' skills to a particular grade level or to enable them to pass the General Educational Development (GED) test (although these achievements were important markers of progress) but to help them develop the knowledge and skills necessary to achieve their own goals and purposes and "to compete in a global economy and exercise the rights and responsibilities of citizenship" (National Education Goals Panel, 1991, Goal 6).

NEW DIRECTIONS FOR ADULT AND CONTINUING EDUCATION, no. 155, Fall 2017 © 2017 Wiley Periodicals, Inc.
Published online in Wiley Online Library (wileyonlinelibrary.com) • DOI: 10.1002/ace.20238

This consistent focus, over the years, on clarifying and addressing the broad range of what adult learners need to know and be able to do in order to meet their own goals is what initially brought me to PIAAC—the Organisation for Economic Cooperation and Development's (OECD) Program for the International Assessment of Adult Competencies. First administered in 2011–12 in 23 countries, including the United States, PIAAC was designed to give the leaders of these nations important information on how well prepared their adult residents were to participate fully in the civic, cultural, and economic life of their countries in the 21st century. Results from PIAAC's three core assessments in literacy, numeracy, and problem solving in technology-rich environments (PS-TRE), when combined with data from its rich and detailed background questionnaire (BQ), provide educators and policymakers with a complex picture of the level and distribution of skills possessed by adults within and across participating countries and their relationship to a diverse array of factors.

Although these results are important, especially from a policy perspective, they are not the focus of this paper.[2] Rather, this paper invites readers to approach PIAAC as I did initially, by learning about the overarching framework that OECD developed to guide its work in defining and selecting key competencies and how that framework, and the definitions of competence it gave rise to in PIAAC, can support a range of purposes that we do not necessarily associate with assessments. At a time when adult education instruction has been largely reframed by an emphasis on decontextualized skill instruction that mirrors K–12 education, a theoretically sound, research-based, and internationally validated framework that focuses on a broader definition of competence—*on what adults can do with the skills they have*—offers an alternative way to approach and answer the question: What is the most effective way to deliver adult literacy education if our goal is to support our students' development and use of literacy to lead successful lives and fully participate in a rapidly changing society?

DeSeCo: Creating an Overarching Framework for Education Indicators

As OECD countries began to feel the effects of globalization in the 1980s and 90s, they became more interested in understanding the economic and social returns on their investments in education. Additionally, the breakup of the Soviet Union, beginning with the fall of the Berlin Wall in 1989, raised questions about what was necessary to prepare citizens of the new republics that emerged for a transition to democracy. In this context, OECD identified a need to ground its empirical work, focused on creating reliable, internationally comparable indicators, in "an overarching, theory-based framework for defining and selecting relevant human competencies necessary for living a successful life in a well-functioning, democratic society" (Rychen & Salganik, 2001, pp. 1, 4). Thus was born Defining and Selecting Key Competencies (DeSeCo), an OECD project coordinated by the Swiss Federal Statistical Office. DeSeCo drew on research from multiple disciplines as well as policy initiatives in 12 OECD countries to arrive at a common vision of what constitutes a "successful life and a well-functioning democratic society" and then to determine what the key competencies are that enable success in "an increasingly interdependent, rapidly changing, and at times conflict-prone world" (Rychen & Salganik, 2003, p. 111).

Asking these foundational questions about what members of advanced, democratic societies need to know and be able to do would enable OECD to look at its current assessment programs, including the Program for International Student Assessment (PISA), to see whether, and to what extent, they focused on competencies that were critical to a successful life. The DeSeCo framework did not attempt to delineate the full range of competencies necessary to achieve the vision it defined; rather, it identified three broad categories of competence related to the demands of modern life: acting autonomously, using tools interactively, and interacting in socially heterogeneous groups.

Elaborating this framework revealed that almost all of OECD's assessments measured competence only in the category "using tools interactively." Although this category does overlap with "acting autonomously" and "interacting in socially heterogeneous groups," there are many other competencies and constellations of competencies that are critical to these other two categories that were not being measured and were not even fully defined. The DeSeCo framework highlighted these other important areas of competence. The assumption was that if countries were truly interested in ensuring that their citizens could lead successful lives, then policymakers would need to commit to expanding their education initiatives to build these competencies, and researchers would have to help understand how to teach and measure them.

To facilitate this policy and research process, the DeSeCo framework included a broad and comprehensive definition of competence itself. According to Heinz Gilomen (2003), the Swiss director of Social and Education Statistics who chaired the DeSeCo project, what was most important in the definition was

the notion that competencies are demand- and action-oriented and are made up of a combination of attitudes, values, knowledge and skills. Competencies are observable in the actions an individual undertakes in particular situations and contexts ... Competence is not a dichotomous quality that a person either does or does not possess. Therefore, it is not a matter of assessing whether an individual does or does not possess a particular competence ... but rather of determining where along the continuum from a low to a high competence level an individual's performance falls. (p. 204)

New Directions for Adult and Continuing Education • DOI: 10.1002/ace

The Impact of DeSeCo on PIAAC

OECD's PIAAC initiative was launched in the context of DeSeCo, with its new, broader definition of competence. In *OECD Skills Outlook* 2013: *First Results from the Survey of Adult Skills*, OECD describes its motivation for launching PIAAC:

> Skills transform lives, generate prosperity and promote social inclusion. Without the right skills, people are kept at the margins of society; technological progress does not translate into economic growth, and enterprises and countries can't compete in today's globally connected and increasingly complex world. Getting the best returns on investment in skills requires good information about the skills that are needed and available in the labour market. It also requires policies that ensure that skills are used effectively to generate better jobs that lead to better lives. To support these goals, the OECD has begun to measure the skills of the adult population. (OECD, 2013, p. 26)

Although the emphasis in this rationale is on economic outcomes, the identification of individual transformation and social inclusion as goals of the measurement initiative gestures toward the three categories of competence in DeSeCo's overarching framework. Similarly, although all three domains of the PIAAC assessment fit squarely in the category of "interacting with tools," the assessment as a whole, including the BQ and Skills Use Module, does address aspects of "acting autonomously" and "interacting in heterogeneous groups." Most important, the Expert Groups charged with developing content frameworks for assessment of each of the three domains adopted the action orientation of the DeSeCo definition of competence.

As a first step toward designing the PIAAC Survey, the International Consortium that oversaw the development of the project identified an international expert group for each of the three assessments. Each group was charged with developing a definition of the domain to be assessed that took into account the history of how the domain had been defined and assessed but that also was congruent with the DeSeCo definition of competence. The domain definition was the core of each content framework and the basis for both item development and guidance on how to conduct the assessment. For example, the PIAAC Numeracy Expert Group (2009) defined its work in this way:

> The conceptualisation of numeracy in an assessment program . . . has to be congruent with the broader notion of "competence." Within OECD, prior work on the Definition and Selection of Competencies project has defined competence as "the ability to meet individual or social demands successfully, or to carry out an activity or task." The DeSeCo view . . . *places at the forefront how individuals function in the face of external demands that may stem from a personal or social context of action. . . . Each competence is built on a combination of interrelated cognitive and practical skills, knowledge (including tacit knowledge), motivation, value orientation,*

New Directions for Adult and Continuing Education • DOI: 10.1002/ace

attitudes, emotions, and other social and behavioral components that together can be mobilised for effective action. (p. 10, author emphasis added)

The definitions of all three PIAAC domains embrace this broader notion of competence. The Literacy Expert Group defined literacy as "understanding, evaluating, using and engaging with written texts to participate in society, to achieve one's goals, and to develop one's knowledge and potential" (PIAAC Literacy Expert Group, 2009, p. 8). The definition of numeracy as "the ability to access, use, interpret, and communicate mathematical information and ideas, in order to engage in and manage the mathematical demands of a range of situations in adult life" (PIAAC Numeracy Expert Group, 2009, p. 20) focuses on the purpose or goal that leads an adult to "try to manage or respond to a numeracy situation" (PIAAC Numeracy Expert Group, 2009, p. 20). In addition, the Expert Group identifies "*attitudes* toward mathematics, *beliefs* about mathematical skills, *habits of mind*, and *prior experiences* involving tasks with mathematical content" as key processes that enable numerate behavior (PIAAC Numeracy Expert Group, 2009, p. 30, author emphasis).

The PS-TRE Expert Group defined their domain as "using digital technology, communication tools and networks to acquire and evaluate information, communicate with others and perform practical tasks" (PIAAC Expert Group on PS-TRE, 2009, p. 9). In deconstructing the definition, the Expert Group states that "the problem solving context means that routine or basic information and communication technology (ICT) skills will not be central to the framework. Instead, PS-TRE will focus on situations that involve the active construction of goals and strategies on the part of the user" (PIAAC Expert Group on PS-TRE, 2009, p. 9). The Expert Group further asserts that goal-setting involves "identifying one's needs or purposes, given the explicit and implicit constraints of a situation" (PIAAC Expert Group on PS-TRE, 2009, p. 12), reminding us that individual goals and purposes are key for this domain as well.

Using PIAAC's Use-Oriented Definition of Competence to Guide Instruction

It is the purposeful focus on what OECD calls " a use-oriented definition of competency" (OECD, 2016, p. 16) that makes the domain definitions in PIAAC assessments so useful to practitioners. Here, "the focus is less on the mastery of certain content (e.g., vocabulary or arithmetic operations) and . . . cognitive strategies *than on the ability to draw on this content and these strategies to successfully perform information-processing tasks in a variety of real-world situations*" (OECD, 2016, p. 16, author emphasis). As a result, these definitions of competence provide a way of conceptualizing practice at the policy, program, and instructional level that values and is responsive to the purposes for learning which adult students bring to programs. Trawick (2017) illustrates this in her discussion of how the PIAAC Literacy Framework can be

Figure 3.1. Model for Contextualized Reading Instruction

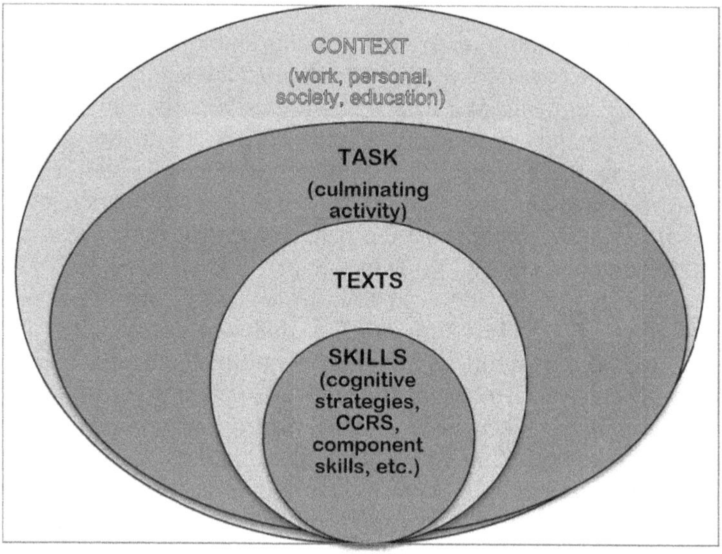

Source: Trawick, 2017, p. 21

used to help programs evaluate how well they meet the real-world needs of their students:

> Together, the purposes and types of text interactions described in PIAAC's definition for literacy offer us a concrete reference point for reflecting on what the vision is for literacy (reading) instruction in our setting ... [They encourage us to ask] are we structuring learning opportunities in reading and wrap-around services for adult learners in ways that transfer to their lives? Practitioners in an adult basic education program might use this definition to revisit the program's mission/vision statement, curriculum, and services to ascertain if the scope of literacy programming they offer supports the purposes for literacy and types of text interactions described in the literacy framework. (p. 7)

The Three-Element Model. The definitions of competence for the three PIAAC domains are particularly useful for programs trying to ensure durable, transferable learning by integrating real-world activities, tasks, and tools (National Research Council, 2012, p. 4). The definitions invite practitioners to frame teaching of component skills and strategies in the context of purposeful learning activities/performance tasks that integrate three key elements:

Context—the situation in which an adult needs to use the skill

Content—the texts, or artifacts, or tools that adults must respond to or engage with when using the skill, and

Cognitive strategies—the processes that adults must bring into play to respond to or use given content in an appropriate manner. (OECD, 2013, p. 59)

Trawick (2017) illustrates (Figure 3.1) how practitioners might integrate these elements in a nested model for contextualized reading instruction. She explains that

PIAAC helps us envision how [the] **skills** [we teach] are used in real-life as we read **texts** in the pursuit of an overarching **task**, situated within an authentic adult **context.** By applying this same organizing principle of nesting and contextualizing to construct learning activities, we can provide students meaningful learning experiences that develop literacy-in-use for long-term retention and transfer. (Trawick, 2017, p. 21, emphasis in original)

Trawick provides multiple examples of how teachers can use this model to construct learning activities appropriate to their students. Each emphasizes the interrelationships of skill, text, task, and context.

Although the Expert Group for Problem-Solving in Technology Rich Environments (PS-TRE) uses slightly different terminology—tasks, technologies, and cognitive dimensions—the three-element model they present involves the same interaction of context/task, content, and cognitive strategies. In this model, learning how to use a particular digital tool is embedded in the context of an activity focused on the purpose for which the tool is needed. This requires the user to activate a set of cognitive strategies appropriate to accomplishing that purpose. In Figure 3.2, Vanek (2017) demonstrates how a teacher might use this model to map a specific digital task.

Task Complexity and the Continuum of Skill Development. Conceptualizing competence in literacy, numeracy, and PS-TRE as the interaction of these three elements—context (task), content (text/technologies), and skill (cognitive strategies)—gives practitioners a simple heuristic they can use to shift instruction from a focus on decontextualized component or skill instruction to a focus on using the targeted components or skills to accomplish real world tasks. One difficulty in making this shift is that the skill development progressions that teachers use in adult programs focus only on knowledge and skills. As a result, they do not provide guidance in how to systematically adjust all the elements of an applied learning or assessment task so that it challenges without overwhelming students. This is a problem that the PIAAC content frameworks address.

For each PIAAC domain, the expert group defined a set of "factors that affect complexity" that address all three elements—task, content, and skill—of applied learning and assessment tasks. Although the original purpose for these complexity factors was to guide the work of task developers creating assessment items for PIAAC, they also provide a set of rules teachers can use

Figure 3.2. Mapping a Level 1 PS-TRE Item to the Three-Element Model

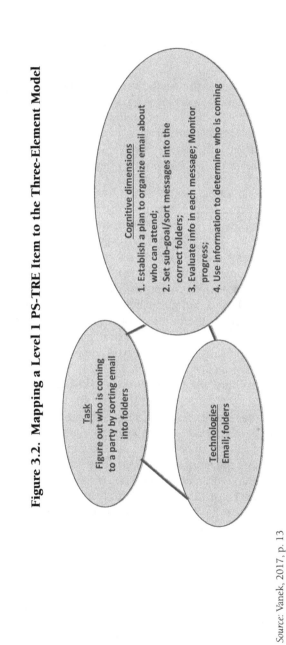

Task
Figure out who is coming to a party by sorting email into folders

Technologies
Email; folders

Cognitive dimensions
1. Establish a plan to organize email about who can attend;
2. Set sub-goal/sort messages into the correct folders;
3. Evaluate info in each message; Monitor progress;
4. Use information to determine who is coming

Source: Vanek, 2017, p. 13

to create or modify real-world tasks for teaching and assessment purposes. In *Using the PIAAC Numeracy Framework to Guide Instruction* (2017, pp. 20–24), Curry focuses on the five factors affecting complexity in the numeracy domain. These include factors teachers think about all the time as they plan instruction, such as the type of operation or skill involved and the number of operations required to solve the problem. But because PIAAC defines competence as the ability to use a skill to accomplish a task, the Numeracy Expert Group also identified factors related to the nature of the task. These include how transparent the problem is, whether the information required to solve the problem is explicit or hidden, whether all the information needed to solve the problem is there, whether there are distractors in the problem, and how complex the mathematical data and action required are (PIAAC Numeracy Expert Group, 2009). Curry (2017) provides a set of questions that can guide teachers in using each of these factors—independently or in concert—to vary the difficulty of tasks to address individual student needs. She also provides several illustrations of the process of modifying tasks that may be helpful to practitioners interested in developing students' capacity to use numeracy skills to address increasingly complex real-life problems (Curry, 2017).

Using PIAAC Data to Support Investment in Literacy

Adult literacy practitioners face an enormously complex task. Their students come to them with diverse educational histories that result in widely disparate sets of learning needs. And they are all in the midst of carrying out multiple roles as parents, workers, and members of communities that every day give rise to new demands for new skills and greater competence. They want and need to be able to use new skills right away. I have tried to show how PIAAC's focus on building applied competence in three domains—literacy, numeracy, and problem solving in technology-rich environments—offers practitioners a way of conceptualizing their work that is congruent with the complexity of students' needs. Of course, practitioners need more than guides like those developed by Curry, Trawick, and Vanek to be successful in their efforts to help students develop greater proficiency in completing the tasks they encounter in their daily lives. Practitioners work in an underfunded system that cannot provide the full-time salaries, professional development resources, or program supports that make it possible for them to make the kind of changes that can produce high-quality, effective instruction that addresses their students' pressing needs. To address this resource problem, practitioners can turn to the results of the PIAAC survey to help make the case for greater investment at the state and national levels in resources, including professional development, that can support building applied competence, as PIAAC defines it, in literacy, numeracy, and problem solving.

The rich trove of data provided by PIAAC can support arguments for more resources for adult basic education by enabling policymakers to understand more about the range and distribution of skills in our adult population and the relationships between skill level and important social and economic indicators, including health status, inequality and social mobility, and earnings and employment status. PIAAC's extensive BQ collects more than the standard demographic data. It includes an unusually comprehensive education and work history that, combined with the assessment data themselves, provides each country with a detailed portrait of the adult population across the range and distribution of literacy, numeracy and digital literacy skills. The Skills Use Module within the BQ collects information on the ways in which respondents use reading, writing, numeracy, and ICT skills at work and at home. In addition, this module collects information relevant to respondents' ability to "act autonomously" and to "interact in socially heterogeneous groups," including how they solve problems and the ways in which they interact with others at work. There are also questions on family literacy and language practices and on respondents' sense of agency, including the extent to which they are able to organize their own activities at work and how they see themselves in relation to the larger society. Thus, although PIAAC assesses only competence relevant to "using tools interactively," it does collect a range of information that will assist in more rigorous definition of indicators for "acting autonomously" and "interacting in socially heterogeneous groups." This is a first step toward more reliable assessments in these areas in the future.

In the United States, the American Institutes for Research (AIR), through a contract with the U.S. Department of Education's National Center for Education Statistics (NCES), has commissioned research studies that analyze PIAAC data to provide support for investments in education as a way to raise wages, address poverty, and reduce intergenerational inequality. Analyses that look at skill level distribution for specific age cohorts or that look at differences between racial and ethnic groups can also help shape better, more carefully targeted, skill development policies and help practitioners understand more about the nature of the complex needs of adults and offer more effective programs.[3] The number and richness of these studies will grow now that the U.S. PIAAC database has been expanded from the 5,000 original respondents to nearly 10,000 respondents through the 2013–14 PIAAC National Supplement & Correctional Study. The supplement oversampled populations for whom our government has a key policy interest: young adults, 16–34; unemployed adults; and older adults, aged 66–75, who were not included in the original study. The Correctional Study surveyed 1,200 incarcerated adults. Researchers can use this expanded database to fine tune the questions they ask and to look in greater detail at various subgroups within the overall population, enabling a deeper understanding of both the populations and possible interventions, which, in turn, can inform better policy and practice.

Conclusion

I began this paper by introducing the theoretical framework for PIAAC's use-oriented definition of competence and exploring how this definition can help practitioners develop adult basic education programs that are better able to help adults achieve their own goals and purposes. The final section of this paper suggests that the evidence PIAAC data provide regarding the many correlations between greater competence and enhanced economic performance and social well-being may encourage policymakers to devote increased resources to adult basic education focused on building applied competence. It is my hope that in both these ways, PIAAC can contribute to achievement of the broad vision that OECD established through its DeSeCo project: a nation—and indeed a world—where more of us are able to live successful lives in well-functioning, democratic societies.

Notes

1. I would like to thank Jaleh Soroui, the director of the PIAAC Project at the American Institutes for Research, for her review of this document and for her support over the 25 years we have worked together to further adult basic education in this country.
2. For more information on PIAAC results visit www.piaacgateway.com or http://www.oecd.org/skills/piaac/publicdataandanalysis/#d.en.408927
3. PIAAC research studies can be retrieved from http://piaacgateway.com/research papers/

References

Curry, Donna. (2017). *Using the PIAAC numeracy framework to guide instruction: An introduction for adult educators*. Washington, DC: American Institutes for Research. Retrieved from http://piaacgateway.com

Gilomen, H. (2003). Conclusions and next steps. In D. S. Rychen, L. H. Salganik, & M. E. McLaughlin (Eds.), *Contributions to the second DeSeCo symposium* (pp. 203–207). Neuchatel, Switzerland: Swiss Federal Statistical Office.

National Education Goals Panel. (1991). *Statement of national education goal 6*. Retrieved from http://govinfo.library.unt.edu/negp/page3-13.htm

National Research Council. (2012). *Improving adult literacy instruction: Developing reading and writing*. Washington, DC: National Academies Press. Retrieved from http://www.nap.edu/catalog/13468/improving-adult-literacy-instruction-developing-reading-and-writing

Organisation for Economic and Community Development. (2013). *OECD skills outlook 2013: First results from the survey of adult skills*. Paris: OECD Publishing. Retrieved from http://doi.org/10.1787/9789264204256-en

Organisation for Economic and Community Development. (2016). *The Survey of Adult Skills: Reader's companion (2nd ed.; OECD Skills Studies)*. Paris: OECD Publishing. Retrieved from http://doi.org/10.1787/9789264258075-en

PIAAC Expert Group on Problem Solving in Technology Rich Environments. (2009). *PIAAC problem solving in technology rich environments: A conceptual framework* (OECD Education Working Paper No. 36). Paris: OECD Publishing. Retrieved from http://www.oecd-ilibrary.org/education/oecd-education-working-papers_19939019?page=3

PIAAC Literacy Expert Group. (2009). *PIAAC literacy: A conceptual framework* (OECD Education Working Paper No. 34). Paris: OECD Publishing. Retrieved from http://www.oecd-ilibrary.org/education/oecd-education-working-papers_19939019?page=3

PIAAC Numeracy Expert Group. (2009). *PIAAC numeracy: A conceptual framework* (OECD Education Working Paper No. 35). Paris: OECD Publishing. Retrieved from http://www.oecd-ilibrary.org/education/oecd-education-working-papers_19939019?page=3

Rychen, D. S., & Salganik, L. H. (Eds.). (2001). *Defining and selecting key competencies.* Göttingen, Germany: Hogrefe & Huber.

Rychen, D. S., & Salganik, L. H. (Eds.). (2003). *Key competencies for a successful life and a well-functioning society.* Göttingen, Germany: Hogrefe & Huber.

Swiss, T. (1976). Adult performance level project. *Journal of Reading, 20*(3), 264–267. Retrieved from http://www.jstor.org/stable/40011482

Trawick, A. R. (2017). *Using the PIAAC literacy framework to guide instruction: An introduction for adult educators.* Washington, DC: American Institutes for Research. Retrieved from http://piaacgateway.com

Vanek, J. (2017). *Using the PIAAC framework for problem solving in technology-rich environments for instruction: An introduction for adult educators.* Washington, DC: American Institutes for Research. Retrieved from http://piaacgateway.com

SONDRA GAYLE STEIN, Ph.D., is a consultant to the PIAAC Project in the Education Division, American Institutes for Research. She is the former senior research associate at the National Institute for Literacy (1993–2004) and national director of its Equipped for the Future Initiative.

New Directions for Adult and Continuing Education • DOI: 10.1002/ace

4

This chapter on high school equivalency describes recent events involved in updating the adult education high school equivalency assessment services and the entrance of additional assessments into the field.

High School Equivalency Assessment and Recognition in the United States: An Eyewitness Account

Lennox McLendon

A mainstay of the adult education system and a stated purpose in every federal adult education bill has been the attainment of a high school equivalent education. In our recent history, the enactment of that purpose has been at a significant turning point. In this chapter, I recount a short history of high school equivalency services, provide an examination of recent significant changes, and relate how the state and local providers addressed those changes. Finally, I conclude with a comment about the potential impact of these changes on the field and for learners.

The origin of the General Education Development (GED®) Test is well known by most adult education practitioners, researchers, and policymakers. It begins with the massive return of GIs from World War II, many of whom had not completed high school. Initially, the GED® Testing Service (GEDTS) at the American Council on Education (ACE) developed a high school equivalency test that would enable assessment and recognition of high school level work for those returning GIs. Soon after, it was made available to all American adults who needed a way to demonstrate high school equivalency skills despite leaving school before graduating. Needless to say, since World War II our society has become more complex and the skills needed to complete high school and enter the world of work have continually increased.

As a result, to maintain the creditability, relevance, and acceptance of the high school equivalency tests, the four or five tests that make up the GED® (the number has varied depending on the test version) have been updated several times since World War II to reflect what high school graduates need to know and be able to do. That "upgrading" of the tests has created considerable angst among both teachers and examinees as each subsequent test version has been widely believed to be more difficult than its predecessor.

New Directions for Adult and Continuing Education, no. 155, Fall 2017 © 2017 Wiley Periodicals, Inc.
Published online in Wiley Online Library (wileyonlinelibrary.com) • DOI: 10.1002/ace.20239

It is worth an aside here to reflect on my belief that the goal of adult education is to enable learners to "prosper." In other words, we are successful when we can help adults qualify for a job with a family sustaining income and more effectively fulfill the range of roles that they seek. In the 1960s when I began teaching adults, in order to "prosper," adult educators felt successful when they had helped learners attain an eighth-grade reading and writing level and the ability to do four-function math computation. To prosper in the 2000s, adults must not only have the math, reading, science, social studies, and English skills needed to transition to postsecondary training and education programs, they must also be able to think critically about and analyze, synthesize, and reconstruct data; conduct complex problem solving; and evaluate, judge, and process text-based information at a much higher level. The Adult Education College and Career Readiness Standards (Pimentel, 2013), which are based on the Common Core State Standards (CCSS), provide the instructional framework for accomplishing those goals and enabling our students to "prosper." However, assessing those more complex skills creates a challenge. In an effort to address this challenge, the GED® was revised and the new version was launched in 2014.

The Need for a Revised GED® Test

The change in 2013–2014 was prompted by several factors. The first was to address the ever-increasing skill levels needed by high school graduates based on the recognition that a high school education is no longer enough to secure a high-demand job with family-sustaining wages (Burning Glass, 2014; Carnevale, Smith, & Strohl, 2010). Thus, a greater emphasis on preparing students for transitions to postsecondary education and training indicated a need for a more rigorous high school equivalency standard that was better aligned with expectations for those contexts. With the passage of the Workforce Improvement Act (WIA) in 1998, Congress was clear that adult education needed not only to improve literacy skills but also to motivate and prepare undereducated, underprepared adults to complete a postsecondary education. WIA promoted adult learners' transition to postsecondary education with a focus on 1- or 2-year occupational certificates as well as associate's degrees. Accordingly, this new focus for both higher academic skills and integration of soft/work readiness skills (critical thinking, problem solving, and the like), and a focus on job preparation required revising and expanding the content of the assessments.

A second impetus to update the tests was the development of the CCSS released in 2010 and adopted by 42 states in subsequent years. The CCSS were developed because the National Governors Association and the Council of Chief State School Officers were concerned that U.S. student skill levels were falling behind students in other countries. This concern was amplified by a growing recognition that the United States is part of a global economy. In order for U.S. workers to compete successfully with

New Directions for Adult and Continuing Education • DOI: 10.1002/ace

workers around the world, higher academic standards became a priority. The CCSS and the subsequent National Adult Education College and Career Readiness Standards (CCRS) were viewed as important mechanisms for accomplishing this goal. To make the GED® tests equivalent to what high school graduates would now be expected to know and be able to do, they needed to be updated.

Critical Decisions in GED® Test Revision

The higher order thinking skills and the academic content imbedded in the CCSS and CCRS did not lend themselves to a paper-and-pencil test. There was considerable sentiment that those skills could best be assessed by a computerized version of a test. That format purported to accommodate measurement of the more complex skill set needed for updated high school equivalency expectations. Discussion of this topic had come up earlier on the agenda of the GEDTS National Advisory Council where I, along with two state directors, represented the state directors of adult education. In addition to state directors of adult education, the council membership represented state chief examiners, relevant professional associations, university faculty, schools, and other stakeholder groups. GEDTS staff used the advisory council to pose new ideas, plan services, and get feedback from their members' constituents. The council members were responsible for communicating information from GEDTS to their constituents. This two-way communication was intended to keep all stakeholders apprised of new developments and plans for the test.

Within the council, even though there was support for the value of a computer-based assessment, there was considerable concern about the cost of making this transition. To some council members, it seemed that a computerized version would naturally be more cost effective than a paper-and-pencil version because the cost of printing and shipping could be eliminated. However, those with expertise in the technology assured us that a computer version was, in fact, much more expensive and would lead to increased examination fees. A second concern about switching to a computer-based test that was voiced in those advisory council meetings concerned the accessibility of computer labs, especially in rural areas. A related concern focused on the cost of establishing accessible computer testing sites. Despite extensive discussions, the council could not reach a conclusion and made no recommendation regarding the wisdom and efficacy of converting the GED® to a computer-based assessment. Much later, however, it became apparent that the leadership of the newly reconfigured GEDTS understood that the National Advisory Council, and all the organizations the members represented, had indeed recommended going to a computerized version. This was a misunderstanding that is an important point in the story.

Another critical decision regarding the test revision concerned the resources needed for development and rollout. The ACE and its affiliate, GEDTS, recognized that the next iteration of the test, especially if there was to be a computer-based version, was going to require greater financial capacity and expertise than they had in house. Thus, the ACE decided to collaborate with a partner to develop the new assessments. Pearson VUE, one of the largest publishers in the world, was selected for this role. Its knowledge and experience in adult education, English for speakers of other languages, and assessment is extensive. It brought both capacity and resources to the partnership. Thus, the GEDTS became a public–private partnership between ACE and Pearson VUE.

One of the first decisions the newly formed GED® Testing Service made about the upcoming revision of the tests was to develop only a computerized version despite there having always been a paper-and-pencil version. It was clear to them that a paper-and-pencil format would limit their ability to assess the complex CCRS competencies. Helping to support that decision, the leadership believed, erroneously, that the National Advisory Council and their constituents had recommended changing to the computer version. Thus, a conundrum was born. On the one hand, evidently the new management team at GEDTS had been told (erroneously) by staff that the adult education field, through the National Advisory Council, had endorsed and supported a computer-only testing system. Therefore, they moved ahead with the development and later announced it to the field. On the other hand, from the field's perspective, especially the state directors', this new partnership had made decisions without consultation from adult educators. The significant increase in cost and concerns regarding rural access to testing were major points of concern. Of greatest concern, however, was the absence of consultation between GEDTS and the state directors regarding the changes. This misunderstanding created much angst throughout the field.

At the request of the state directors, in May 2012 their leadership met with GEDTS leadership with the purpose of resolving issues related to the new format. At that meeting the GEDTS leadership learned, contrary to what they had been told earlier by staff, that the Advisory Council, and therein the state directors, had not recommended a computer-based test. That information was confirmed by a GEDTS staff member who was a former state director and, in that role, had been a member of the advisory committee. The discussion then turned to opportunities to rectify the misunderstanding. However, it was too late to reconsider plans to implement the computer-only assessment.

Impact of the New GED® Test on the Field

A number of events and reactions can occur with the introduction of an upgraded assessment instrument such as the revised GED®. One is that it can cause surges in test taking in the year before and dramatic drops in the first years after it is launched. For example, when the tests were upgraded in 2002, there was much encouragement by adult educators for adults to finish incomplete test batteries and to solicit additional examinees before the tests were changed (and made more difficult). As a result, there was a surge of test taking before the release of the new version of the test. This pattern is illustrated

New Directions for Adult and Continuing Education • DOI: 10.1002/ace

by the fact that there were approximately 748,000 test takers in 2000 and 980,000 in 2001. However, perhaps because the pool of potential examinees had been drained by the previous year's push and because there was trepidation about the difficulty of the new test version, the number of examinees dropped significantly in 2002 to 510,000 (GED Testing Service, 2014).

Fortunately, each subsequent year, the number of examines increased as fears about the new, harder tests waned and programs and staff became better prepared to help learners be successful. However, a similar surge and dip occurred around the 2014 revision of the test (GED Testing Service, 2014). Although 743,000 sat for the test in 2013, that number dropped to 223,000 in 2014, the first year of the new test. However, it should be noted that some decrease in the number of GED® test takers can be attributed to the entry of two competitors in the high school equivalency arena, which is described in more detail in the next section. There were a total of 315,000 test takers when statistics from all three tests are combined.

The development of the new test encountered many hurdles and considerable pushback. As discussed previously, one area of considerable tension related to the transition to computer-only test administration. Not only did some adult education state directors resent the decision because they felt they were not consulted, but many were concerned about the practical challenges of changing to a computer-based assessment. In rural areas of many states, there were no computer labs in which they could administer the tests, and they did not have the funds to create them. These concerns were exacerbated with the receipt of the specifications for Pearson VUE computer labs including facility requirements, technical requirements, and photo/video requirements. These specifications made upgrading or creating computer labs to meet the required standards so that they could accommodate test takers additionally onerous. Even in the urban/suburban programs, there was resistance because of the costs involved in meeting these requirements.

In addition to pushback related to the test going paperless, another issue that arose regarded the nature of the newly formed partnership between the ACE and Pearson. Even though the name, GED® Testing Service, remained the same, many practitioners were concerned that the provider of the GED® had changed from a nonprofit (ACE) to a private, for-profit company (Pearson VUE). In actuality, the new GEDTS is a public–private partnership between ACE and Pearson. It was unclear whether that partnership made GEDTS a nonprofit or a private company. That lack of clarity coupled with the significant increase in assessment fees further contributed to apprehension in the field.

New Entrants in the High School Equivalency Assessment Arena

These concerns opened the door for other entities to enter a market that had, until this time, no competition. As a result, two other providers stepped in: the Educational Testing Service (ETS) and the California Test Bureau (CTB), then a part of McGraw-Hill. Each developed a computerized, as well as a paper and pencil, high school equivalency test. ETS developed the High School Equivalency Test (HiSET) and CTB developed the Test Assessing Secondary Completion (TASC). Both developers stated that their tests were based on the CCSS and the College and Career Readiness Standards.

Multiple providers of high school equivalency testing posed a procurement issue in many states. For example, if there is only one vendor of a product, as there had been for high school equivalency testing until now, the state can do a "sole source" justification to contract with only that vendor. If there are multiple vendors, most state procurement regulations require the state office to go out for bids. With the entry of ETS and CTB into the market, most states were no longer allowed to sole source the high school equivalency assessment. Because of the concern about computer testing accessibility, especially in rural areas, many of those requests for proposals included requirements for both computer and paper-and-pencil tests; the GEDTS was unable to bid in those states. At least in part as a result of concern about the computer-based testing issue, some states adopted two or all three tests.

In addition to the three standardized tests now available, there are other ways for adults to attain a high school diploma. The National External Diploma Program (NEDP) "is an applied performance assessment system that assesses the high school level skills of adults and out-of-school youth. The NEDP evaluates the reading, writing, math, and workforce readiness skills of participants in life and work contexts" (CASAS, 2017, para. 1). NEDP, now supported by CASAS, is used in 84 programs in eight states. Also, many states have a high school completion program where adult student earn Carnegie Units and graduate with a "regular" high school diploma. These programs often require "seat time," making them a viable option for adult students who are only two or three units short of meeting high school graduation requirements and have the time to invest or who do not want an equivalency but rather a "real" diploma. In addition, states may offer a variety of channels for adults to earn a high school diploma. For example, in Wisconsin students have five options including passing the GED® tests and completing additional requirements in citizenship, health, career awareness, and employability skills; attaining 22 high school credits including 11.5 specific credits along with a specified number of postsecondary credits; or having a foreign high school or postsecondary diploma and U.S. citizenship or proficiency in language and literacy skills and a passing grade in a citizenship course.

Ramping Up for New High School Equivalency Assessments

Facing confusion related to the rapid changes to high school equivalency assessment, the adult education state directors' national organization (the National Adult Education Professional Development Consortium [NAEPDC]) created a High School Equivalency Workgroup to explore options and provide states with a forum to share information about how to proceed. To

New Directions for Adult and Continuing Education • DOI: 10.1002/ace

that end, they published several resources on the NAEPDC website. The first is a matrix identifying the tests selected by each state as well as how much they are charging for testing (http://www.naepdc.org/Documents/NAEPDC-HSE010116.pdf). A second web resource includes samples of the requests for proposals that states used to solicit bids from test developers (http://naepdc.org/RFP_RFI.html). Third, the webpage also captured sample changes in state statutes reflecting the multiple testing services now available (http://naepdc.org/State_Statute_Changes.html). This was necessary because the word "GED" was included in many federal and state statutes because for decades the GED® had been the only high school equivalency assessment. Because other assessments were now allowed, the "GED" language in state statutes had to be changed to "high school equivalency."

In addition to devoting time and energy to creating a structure and process for administering the new high school equivalency tests, state and local programs were faced with analyzing the content of the new tests, training teachers to prepare students for those tests and creating curricula for the students to use. Within the state agencies and local programs intense efforts were undertaken to respond effectively to the new version of the assessment. Adult educators busily, if not frantically, examined the specifications of the new tests and professional development to help teachers respond was provided. Book publishers adapted test preparation materials so that they would be aligned with the requirements of the new tests. However, 80% of the adult education teachers in this country are part time. Preparing a workforce of predominantly part-time staff for such a significant instructional change is a challenge.

In 2000, when the GED® test was previously updated and the GED® was managed by the nonprofit ACE and was the only high school equivalency assessment, the U.S. Department of Education funded nationwide transition training for the states, and NAEPDC helped design and deliver that training. However, in 2014 when the GED® was now the product of a public–private partnership and there were other providers, the U.S. Department of Education could no longer support such an effort. Thus, NAEPDC raised private funds to develop and implement a national training institute for state staff that was aligned with the CCRS and, therefore, all high school equivalency tests. The institute focused on professional development and instructional strategies to help adult educators prepare students to successfully attain a high school credential, regardless of the assessment for which they would sit.

Adult educators continue to review instructional test preparation materials produced by publishers who have specialized in this area, develop their own curricula specific to the new assessments, and train instructors as a means of preparing students to demonstrate their high school equivalency skills. A full-bodied professional development and instructional response to the new assessments, coupled with the implementation of the College and Career Readiness Standards, will take some time to completely develop and respond to effectively. As Will Rogers said, "Even if you are on the right track, you'll get run over if you just sit there." Adult educators have much work ahead of them but it is hoped they are on the right track.

The skills adults need to qualify for high-demand jobs involve not only substantial academic skills but also critical thinking, analysis and synthesis, problem solving, and a variety of other higher order thinking skills. Effectively assessing and documenting those skills with reliability and validity is a challenge for any test developer. The field now has three vendors competing for the market. Each of the test developers claim that their assessment is based on the College and Career Readiness Standards. With this element in common, questions regularly arise regarding which test best measures student skills, which one has the highest pass rates, whether states should take up one, two, or all three assessments, and what is best for learners. Some states are planning to adopt all three tests and gather data regarding the quality of each. However, that will take some time and a true comparison may require the same student taking two or even three tests in order to compare. The road ahead is still unclear.

Conclusion

In summary, all the events and options described in this paper are the result of the field wanting to provide a reliable and beneficial way to document adults' skills to prepare them for their work, family, and community roles and responsibilities. However, the issues related to the recent change in the high school equivalency assessments remind us of the need for good information and communications throughout our field. One simple misunderstanding created significant tension throughout the country and substantial change regarding stakeholder relationships and the very assessment system itself.

The jury is out on whether three high school equivalency tests will prove to be beneficial to adult learners. Competition is often a good thing. However, our students do not need any barriers or hindrances on their path. Our focus should be on creating stepping stones from any stumbling block. No doubt, our society will continue to become more complex and the assessments will have to be updated again. However, there is some relief in knowing we will not have to go through a total test revision process again. As it is explained by test developers, it is easy to upgrade computerized tests on the fly—unlike the printed test booklets of old. If our society norms hold true, the competition will provide us better products and improved services for our students.

References

Burning Glass. (2014). *How demand for a bachelor's degree is reshaping the workforce.* Retrieved from http://burning-glass.com/wp-content/uploads/Moving_the_Goalposts.pdf

CASAS. (2017). National External Diploma Program (NEDP). Retrieved from http://www.casas.org/nedp

Carnevale, A. P., Smith, N., & Strohl, J. (2010). *Help wanted: Projections of jobs and education requirements through 2018*. Washington, DC: Georgetown University, Center on Education and the Workforce. Retrieved from https://cew.georgetown.edu/wp-content/uploads/2014/12/fullreport.pdf

GED Testing Service. (2014). *2013 annual statistical report on the GED® Test*. Washington, DC: American Council on Education. Retrieved from http://www.gedtestingservice.com/uploads/files/5b49fc887db0c075da20a68b17d313cd.pdf

Pimentel, S. (2013). *College and Career Readiness Standards*. Washington, DC: U.S. Department of Education.

DR. LENNOX MCLENDON *has over 40 years' experience in adult education as a teacher (ABE, ESL, Adult High School), local director, state staff, state director, graduate school faculty, and manager of two national adult education state director organizations. He recently retired and does occasional consultant work.*

5

This chapter discusses a range of issues that together paint a picture of the impact, potential, and challenges of using digital technologies in adult education.

Technology for Innovation and Change in Adult Basic Skills Education

David J. Rosen, Jenifer B. Vanek

Technology has changed the way we live and what is required for full participation in economic and civic life. Our complex, technology-rich world includes family, community, and work interactions that require daily application of digital literacy and strong problem-solving skills. Adult basic skills practitioners need to understand how the digital world affects learners and how technology can enrich learning; practitioners must also provide ample opportunity for learners to build technology skills for formal and informal learning, including literacy, language, and other basic skills, and in further education and training.

The Digital Landscape

To set the stage for understanding the impact and potential for technology in adult basic skills education, we begin by describing access, use, and the potential impact of digital technologies in learning, work, and daily life, aspects that shape the digital landscape for adult learners.

Increased Access to the Internet with Smartphones. Originally, the so-called "digital divide" pointed to a gap between those who could and could not access digital technology; it now refers to the gap between those who can and cannot use accessible technologies to communicate and access information (Wei & Hindman, 2011). The prevalence of smartphones has complicated this understanding of the digital divide. A 2015 Tyton Partners study found that "approximately 55% to 75% of the 4.1 million adult education students in programs today, own smartphones" (Newman, Rosbash, & Sarkisian, 2015, p. 17). Further, a Pew study showed that smartphone use is growing, just as home broadband access has plateaued, for all demographic categories (Horrigan & Duggan, 2015).

These studies suggest that adult learners can access information from home, work, or places that offer public Wi-Fi. Potentially, with greater

NEW DIRECTIONS FOR ADULT AND CONTINUING EDUCATION, no. 155, Fall 2017 © 2017 Wiley Periodicals, Inc.
Published online in Wiley Online Library (wileyonlinelibrary.com) • DOI: 10.1002/ace.20240

Internet access through smartphones, adult learners can use smartphone technology for learning. However, access to regular and reliable broadband, access to computers (needed for many learning and formal assessment tasks), and competence in using digital devices to evaluate information or to solve problems at work, in learning, or in daily living are highly variable. This variance has created a new digital divide and should be of special concern to adult basic education (ABE) practitioners.

Technology for Problem Solving at Work and in Daily Living. Problem-solving skills have always been important in daily life; technology offers new, and sometimes better, ways to solve problems. Although adult learners can benefit from information that is literally at their fingertips any time through their phones, these devices are truly useful for problem solving only if users know how to efficiently search for information and judge its relevance and quality. Some workplaces now offer just-in-time assistance to solve work-related problems by instantly connecting employees with experts to whom they can send text, images, or videos of a problem at hand, but the success of the assistance depends on the ability to effectively text, do word processing, email, and take and send still and video images. Work-related and other problem solving may also benefit from digital tools that organize tasks such as spreadsheets, databases, visual flowcharts, and mapping tools, but these, too, require knowledge of the relevant tools and knowing when and how to deploy them most effectively.

Using these resources may also require solving problems with the technology itself (Reder, 2015). For example, when phoning on a mobile device, a cellular network may not be available, or users might be notified that they have reached their monthly data limit. In such cases, one needs to solve a technology problem to complete a task. The Organisation for Economic Cooperation and Development's (OECD) study of adult skills—the Program for International Assessment of Adult Competencies (PIAAC)—includes a domain that defines a process for such problem solving. Problem Solving in Technology Rich Environments (PS-TRE) is a domain that measures proficiency needed for successful engagement in 21st century living; it requires identifying tasks to be completed, planning or crafting a process for completing the tasks, and choosing appropriate technologies to use at the right time (OECD, 2013). Today the need for employing PS-TRE is constant. Because of the introduction of technology, what might often have been a familiar task may now be one requiring a new solution. For example, communication with a child's teachers may be accomplished more efficiently now through email or an online "parent portal" than by a phone call, but for this communication a parent will need more technology problem-solving skills than those needed to simply use a telephone.

Technology and Cultural Identity. Our highly technological society affects how we understand our place in the world. For example, the rapid development and adoption of online communication technologies over the past 20 years has broadened the number and kind of people with whom we can interact. For immigrants, refugees, and migrants, this means leaving home need not mean disconnecting from their homelands or ending their native language use (Blommaert, 2010). Many adult learners are migrants whose identity and language use are shaped by this transnational reality; they are affected by digitally mediated forms of participation in social networks. Internet skills can help migrant adult learners find information and accomplish tasks by using local resources and drawing on transnational family networks (Noguerón-Liu, 2013). Additionally, supporting the maintenance of home language through sustained connections abroad can have a positive impact on their identity and on their English language and literacy development in the United States (García & Wei, 2013).

Technology for Reading. For adult learners who may be native speakers of English but who have difficulty reading or writing, improving literacy with reading instruction using technology offers a way to improve reading skills without publicly disclosing their reading or writing deficits. Portable digital devices can provide literacy instruction for people who cannot, or choose not to, attend ABE programs, but who may be able to improve their skills through distance learning or through a blended model involving a combination of online courses or apps and face-to-face instruction.

For adults with severe reading disabilities who may not be improving their skills through traditional instruction, technology offers a means to get information from digital text through "auding." This term, first used by researcher Don Brown (1950), refers to having written text read out loud, often now by an automated text reader, who sometimes "auds" at speeds that untrained listeners could not comprehend (Teitell, 2015); adults who practice listening at these speeds may be able to aud text as fast as good readers can read in the traditional way. Although some may not regard auding as reading, if those who aud can get meaning from text as quickly as expert traditional readers, then we may need to accept a broader definition of reading that includes auding as well as decoding written text. Auding has long been an acceptable practice for those with sight disabilities; perhaps it is time to accept this practice for those who have severe reading disabilities.

Technology for Broader Access to Information. For many ABE learners, the Internet offers information in print and video about topics, places, ideas, and opportunities to which they frequently say they would not otherwise have had access. The Internet, as learners sometimes have described it to the authors of this chapter, opens their eyes to new possibilities and allows them to see themselves in new ways. There is also recent research suggesting that African Americans, Latinos, and those who have no college education are more likely than Whites, Asians, and those with a college degree to use the Internet to broaden their social networks (Gonzales, 2015).

Technology, Literacies, and Lifewide Learning

Leveraging the power of digital technologies requires some digital literacy. Adult educators can prepare learners to use technology by teaching digital literacy skills and then supporting learners as they draw on those skills in other learning. Teachers can begin by considering the skills required when using smartphones, a computer, and the Internet and then reflect on how these skills or literacies might be used or applied in daily life and learning (e.g., finding a job; communicating with teachers; or doing online research, writing, or presenting to carry out learning projects).

Technology and Digital Literacies. To better understand the impact of technology on learners' lives and how to best support its use in education, teachers should understand what is meant by "digital literacy." The U.S. Department of Education's Office of Career, Technical, and Adult Education (OCTAE) defines digital literacy as "the skills associated with using technology to enable users to find, evaluate, organize, create, and communicate information" (U.S. Department of Education, 2015, p. 1). It has also been described as "New Literacies" (Buckingham, 1993) because of the expanded notions of text that technology creates. For example, Lankshear and Knobel (2013) point out that emerging technologies such as CD-ROM and video games created new contexts for interacting with text and thus expanded literacy activities. These New Literacies, Buckingham (1993) suggested, were as much a literate practice as those occurring through interactions with traditional text. The skills adult learners need for successful use of computers and the Internet are shaped by a growing flood of visual and text information available on the Internet; hence, it is worth drawing attention to the plural aspect of the term "literacies."

The "literacies" represent new ways of reading and writing required for communicating; searching for, evaluating, or making use of information or engaging digital technology for daily tasks. For example, photo-visual literacy requires reading for meaning of shapes and symbols found in digital media or successfully anticipating the action initiated by clicking on an icon in a digital environment (Eshet-Alkalai, 2004). Lateral (hypermedia) literacy is a nonlinear means by which one accesses information, knowing that clicking on text highlighted by a color-formatted font will navigate the user to a new webpage, video, or other piece of digital information (Jones-Kavalier & Flannigan, 2006). Additionally, remix, or reproduction literacy, supports editing digital texts and images to create original works shared in a digital environment (Jones-Kavalier & Flannigan, 2006; Markham, 2013).

Digital technologies have also created new requirements for higher level skills. For example, information literacy is the ability to make use of multimedia technology to find, evaluate, make use of, and share information using digital technologies (Lankshear & Knobel, 2013). Network literacy, which has become relevant given the predominance of online social networking, involves developing the skills to create and learn through personal networks (Pegrum, 2010). Network literacy might involve knowing how to nurture one's digital social networks and which networks to use for different tasks (e.g., LinkedIn for work and Snapchat for friends and family). Arguably, proficiency across these literacies supports full participation in many aspects of daily life.

New Directions for Adult and Continuing Education • DOI: 10.1002/ace

Lifewide Learning. Adults living in a technologically rich society call upon these literacies in many contexts, so thinking about learning as a lifewide activity can help us better support learners' development. This view recognizes that learning is not confined to school or formal education or training programs but occurs in activities across multiple social settings as one embraces opportunities to grow or succeed within them (Jackson, 2011). Norman Jackson, who developed a lifewide curriculum to prepare postsecondary students to live in a technologically complex "informational world" (2011, p. 14), writes that lifewide learning differs from lifelong learning in its breadth. "Learning can no longer be viewed as a ritual that one engages in during only the early part of one's life with an occasional refresher course to cater for incidental needs during adulthood" (p. 7). Jackson (2012) suggests a curricular approach of contextualized experiential learning that pushes beyond teaching "about" something to providing opportunities for learners to learn by doing and to take action with knowledge. In adult education, we can see examples of lifewide learning when technology instruction responds to learner interests and needs and is project based. Teachers could present activities that require learners to use knowledge in contexts where they need to draw on what they have learned and monitor how successfully they can apply it in real-world tasks.

Using Technology to Support Federal Adult Basic Education Learning Priorities

Technology can help ABE programs attend to federal policy priorities. For example, OCTAE has determined that digital literacy is a priority for ABE programs funded under the Workforce Innovation and Opportunity Act (WIOA). Specifically, (a) digital literacy is viewed as an allowable workforce preparation activity and a component of a newly allowed activity, Integrated Education and Training; (b) states' technical assistance to education providers can include support for technology integration, development of technology and translation applications, and distance education; and (c) states' choice of program recipients for federal funding must be based on, among other things, the extent to which they employ technology-rich programming (U.S. Department of Education, 2015).

Technology as a priority is also evident in the U.S. Department of Education's Adult Education College and Career Readiness (CCR) standards, where it is included as part of preparation for science, technology, engineering, and mathematics and also specifically noted in writing and math standards. CCR Standard 6, on writing and publishing, calls for proficiency using the Internet and other technologies "to produce and publish writing and to interact and collaborate with others" (Pimentel, 2013, p. 105). It articulates several subskills including keyboarding, collaborative use of digital writing and publishing tools, linking to and citing sources, and sharing writing using the Internet. A CCR Mathematics Standard includes items that point to the potential of technology tools to solve mathematical problems, compare data, and better understand mathematical concepts.

Challenges in Using Technology in Adult Basic Skills Education

Despite its importance in modern adult life and its alignment with current adult education policy and goals, persistent challenges in using technology may be more pronounced in ABE than in other education sectors because of dramatic underfunding. This is evident in the difficulty ABE programs face providing access to up-to-date hardware and software and appropriate online curricula, which are often beyond budget. Among other challenges, the most critical are availability of high-quality professional development, a paucity of models and research on effective uses of technology in the classroom, and limitations in current state and federal policy.

Professional Development Challenges. Sustained in-depth professional development, coaching, and ongoing technical assistance are needed for teachers to use technology effectively in their classrooms and in blended or fully online learning models (Buabeng-Andoh, 2012; Desimone & Garet, 2015). Without this and technical assistance, access to technology, and paid professional time to develop and practice newly learned skills and knowledge, technology integration will be minimal at best. Teachers and administrators also need to learn how to evaluate and use hardware and software that can effectively address instructional and programmatic challenges.

There are some excellent examples of this work. The Arizona Department of Education's Adult Education Services has committed to broad implementation of blended learning in a range of programs by providing not only access to online curricula but also opportunities for yearlong professional development for teachers and program administrators on effective instructional models in blended learning programs. In Texas, the Adult Education and Literacy Department of the Texas Workforce Commission supports teachers by providing a diverse range of professional development, including regular 30-minute webinars on using new technology and longer term self-paced online learning to improve their use of technology in classroom and distance learning. Both states draw on resources from the IDEAL Consortium, a World Education, Inc., EdTech Center project that provides professional development materials and technical assistance on blended and online learning.

Adult Basic Skills Education Research. Sound models for professional development and use of technology in ABE classrooms rely on high-quality research. However, the body of research in this area is quite thin (Litster et al., 2014). This explains why there are limited instructional models defining effective use of technology in ABE classrooms. The limited body of work that has been published is difficult for ABE teachers to access at no cost, unless they are affiliated with postsecondary institutions. Further, teachers might not view research articles as the most relevant way to inform practice, preferring instead to rely more on each other or professional development for information

New Directions for Adult and Continuing Education • DOI: 10.1002/ace

(Price & Kirkwood, 2014). Price and Kirkwood found that much available research is based on measuring exit behaviors and assessment results but that instructors were more apt to change instructional practice in response to descriptive findings gleaned from qualitative studies. Teachers' preference for qualitative studies stands in contrast to the research privileged by funding and policy decisions, which tends to be quantitative, experimental design research. We support a broader view of what constitutes relevant research that includes longitudinal or mixed methods research with quantitative measures of learner growth over time complemented by qualitative evidence of learner experience or teacher practice.

Recently, OCTAE has come to appreciate the importance of longitudinal studies of participation in adult basic education (Reder, 2015) and the positive impact that this participation, for at least 100 hours of instruction, can have on participants' lifelong earnings. However, to date, there has only been one longitudinal study of participation in adult basic skills learning conducted in the United States, limited to participants in Portland, Oregon (http://lsal.pdx.edu/). To better understand the outcomes—and impact—of participation in adult basic skills instruction, and in particular the use of technology in instruction and learning, the field must have more longitudinal, qualitative and quantitative data.

The SRI Technologies for Adult Basic Literacies Evaluation (TABLE) study is an example of a promising mixed-methods study. This large-scale, 2-year investigation of online learning curricula in ABE settings explored the use of five online curricula developed for ABE in 28 sites in 12 states, including approximately 80 instructors and 2,000 students. Much of the data were gathered through quantitative methods; however, the study also included interview and observational data (Murphy et al., 2017). These data, and the findings they support, can be mined for descriptions of effective program implementation and instructional practice. Further, the TABLE study shows the potential to serve as a model of mixed-methods research that can lead to the development of useful instructional approaches.

Policy Challenges. The final area of challenge includes the need for federal and state policy to more explicitly address—and to provide funding for—the integration of technology in ABE. Federal funding has not increased for adult basic education under the major federal legislation (i.e., WIOA), and most state funding has not increased; in some states, for example New Jersey, and Pennsylvania, state funding has dramatically decreased (Rosen, 2016). Further, because some states and programs may interpret WIOA as emphasizing integrated education and training and preparation for postsecondary education, this may cause a shift of resources away from serving learners at the most basic levels to those who are preparing for college and careers, leaving further behind those who have the lowest literacy and English language learning skills (Jacobson, 2016; Pickard, 2016; Vanek, 2016). Such a shift in the use of resources to college and career-focused lifelong learning would be to the detriment of lifewide learning that includes knowledge and skills that benefit individual and family health, civic participation, and skills that enable parents to help their children develop reading readiness and succeed in school.

Conclusion

Technology literally means a set of tools; however, in this context we refer specifically to digital tools. The 1995 Rand Corporation paper, *Universal Access to E-mail Feasibility and Societal Implications* (Anderson, Bikson, Law, & Bridger, 1995), focused on who had access to these tools, namely well-to-do and/or well-educated individuals, but argued that within a decade the tools, or at least email, would be widespread in U.S. society. Within a year, "digital divide" was used by members of the National Telecommunications and Information Administration to refer to a disparity in access to email and to the Internet. However, nearly everyone now has access to the Internet. Yet the new digital divide still separates individuals by social class and educational opportunity. Those with more resources have more convenient, faster, and more reliable access; better educated individuals have more facility in using digital tools for problem solving and for lifelong and lifewide learning. ABE learners were typically on the other side of the 1990s digital divide and, although the access divide has narrowed, they are often still on the other side of the new digital use divide.

To address this, educators must teach adult learners digital literacy and problem-solving skills and work to maximize opportunities to use these skills in learning and other parts of their lives. Although teachers, program managers, and policymakers may agree on this agenda for preparing learners to participate in our society, there is much work to be done through policy and professional development to ensure that this is an attainable reality.

References

Anderson, R., Bikson, T., Law, S., & Bridger, M. (1995). *Universal access to e-mail: Feasibility and societal implications*. Santa Monica, CA: RAND Corporation. Retrieved from http://www.rand.org/pubs/monograph_reports/MR650.html.

Blommaert, J. (2010). *The sociolinguistics of globalization*. Cambridge: Cambridge University Press.

Brown, D. (1950). Teaching aural English. *English Journal, 39*(3), 128–136.

Buabeng-Andoh, C. (2012). Factors influencing teachers' adoption and integration of information and communication technology into teaching: A review of the literature. *International Journal of Education and Development Using Information and Communication Technology, 8*(1), 136–155.

Buckingham, D. (1993, May). Towards new literacies, information technology, English and media education. *English and Media Magazine*, 20–25.

Desimone, L. M., & Garet, M. S. (2015). Best practices in teachers' professional development in the United States. *Psychology, Society & Education, 7*(3), 252–263.

Eshet-Alkalai, Y. (2004). Digital literacy: A conceptual framework for survival skills in the digital era. *Journal of Educational Multimedia and Hypermedia, 13*(1), 93–106. Retrieved from http://www.editlib.org/p/4793

García, O., & Wei, L. (2013). *Translanguaging: Language, bilingualism and education*. New York: Palgrave Macmillan.

Gonzales, A. L. (2015, January). Disadvantaged minorities' use of the Internet to expand their social networks. *Communication Research Journal*. Retrieved from http://crx.sagepub.com/content/early/2015/01/12/0093650214565925.abstract

Horrigan, J. B., & Duggan, M. (2015). *Home broadband 2015*. Washington, DC: Pew Research Center. Retrieved from http://www.pewInternet.org/files/2015/12/Broadband-adoption-full.pdf

Jacobson, E. (2016). Workforce development rhetoric and the realities of 21st century capitalism. *Literacy and Numeracy Studies*, 24(1), 3–22. http://doi.org/10.5130/lns.v24i1.4898

Jackson, N. J. (2011). The lifelong and lifewide dimensions of living, learning, and developing. In N. J. Jackson (Ed.), *Learning for a complex world: Lifewide concept of learning, education and personal development* (pp. 1–21). Bloomington, IN: AuthorHouse.

Jackson, N. J. (2012). Lifewide learning: History of an idea. In N. J. Jackson & B. Cooper (Eds.), *Lifewide learning, education, & personal development* (pp. 1–30). Retrieved from http://www.lifewideebook.co.uk/conceptual.html

Jones-Kavalier, B., & Flannigan, S. (2006). Connecting the digital dots: Literacy of the 21st century. *Educause Quarterly*, 29(2), 8–10.

Lankshear, C. & Knobel, M. (2013). Social and cultural studies of new literacies from an educational perspective. In C. Lankshear & M. Knobel (Eds.), *A new literacies reader: Educational perspectives* (pp. 1–19). New York: Peter Lang.

Litster, J., Mallows, D., Morris, M., Redman, R., Benefield, P., & Grayson, H. (2014). *Learning technology in adult English, maths and ESOL/ELT provision: An evidence review* (BIS Research Paper No. 196). London: Department for Business, Innovation and Skills. Retrieved from https://www.gov.uk/government/publications/learning-technology-review-of-english-maths-english-for-speakers-of-other-languages-and-english-language-training

Markham, A. (2013, February 3). What is remix? A research method oriented sketch. Retrieved from http://www.markham.Internetinquiry.org/2013/02/what-is-remix-a-research-method-oriented-sketch/

Murphy, R., Bienkowski, M., Bhanot, R., Wang, S., Wetzel, T., House, A., ... Van Brunt, J. (2017). *Evaluating digital learning for adult basic literacy and numeracy*. Menlow Park: SRI International. Retrieved from https://www.sri.com/sites/default/files/publications/evaluating-digital-learning_1.pdf

Newman, A., Rosbash, T., & Sarkisian, L. (2015). *Learning for life: The opportunity for technology to transform adult education*. Boston, MA: Tyton Partners. Retrieved from http://tytonpartners.com/tyton-wp/wp-content/uploads/2015/03/Learning-for-Life_The-Oppty-for-Tech-to-Transform-Adult-Education_March-20151.pdf

Noguerón-Liu, S. (2013). Access to technology in transnational social fields: Simultaneity and digital literacy socialization of adult immigrants. *International Multilingual Research Journal*, 7(1), 33–48. https://doi.org/10.1080/19313152.2013.746801

Organisation for Economic Cooperation and Development. (2013). *OECD skills outlook 2013: First results from the survey of adult skills*. Paris: OECD Publishing. Retrieved from http://www.oecd-ilibrary.org/education/oecd-skills-outlook-2013_9789264204256-en

Pegrum, M. (2010). "I link, therefore I am": Network literacy as a core digital literacy. *E-Learning and Digital Media*, 7(4), 346–354. https://doi.org/10.2304/elea.2010.7.4.346

Pickard, A. (2016). Forum: WIOA and adult learning. *Journal of Research & Practice for Adult Literacy, Secondary & Basic Education*, 5(2), 50–55.

Pimentel, S. (2013). *College and career readiness standards for adult education*. Washington, DC: U.S. Department of Education, Office of Vocational and Adult Education. Retrieved from http://lincs.ed.gov/publications/pdf/CCRStandardsAdultEd.pdf

Price, L., & Kirkwood, A. (2014). Using technology for teaching and learning in higher education: A critical review of the role of evidence in informing practice. *Higher Education Research & Development, 33*(3), 549–564. https://doi.org/10.1080/07294360.2013.841643

Reder, S. (2015). *Digital inclusion and digital literacy in the United States: A portrait from PIAAC's Survey of Adult Skills*. Washington, DC: American Institutes for Research. Retrieved from http://static1.squarespace.com/static/51bb74b8e4b0139570ddf020/t/551c3e82e4b0d2fede6481f9/1427914370277/Reder_PIAAC.pdf

Rosen, D. (2016). *Increasing funding for adult basic skills through well-organized, strategic, never-let-go advocacy*. Webinar sponsored by the New Jersey Association for Lifelong Learning. Retrieved from youtube.com/watch?v=nZV4N0AMlGk&feature=youtu.be

Teitell, B. (2015, November 6). More and more audio enthusiasts hitting fast forward. *Boston Globe*. Retrieved from http://www.bostonglobe.com/lifestyle/2015/11/05/how-speed-listening-became-new-speed-reading/bvvDL7Iul2zoPEExpE80dK/story.html?s_campaign=email_BG_TodaysHeadline&s_campaign=

U.S. Department of Education, Office of Career, Technical, and Adult Education. (2015). *Integrating technology in WIOA, March 2015 fact sheet*. Retrieved from http://www2.ed.gov/about/offices/list/ovae/pi/AdultEd/integrating-technology.pdf

Vanek, J. (2016). De facto language policy in legislation defining adult basic education in the United States. *Language Policy, 15*(1), 71–95. http://doi.org/10.1007/s10993-015-9356-0

Wei, L., & Hindman, D. B. (2011). Does the digital divide matter more? Comparing the effects of new media and old media use on the education-based knowledge gap. *Mass Communication and Society, 14*(2), 216–235. Retrieved from http://doi.org/10.1080/15205431003642707

DR. DAVID J. ROSEN *was from 1986 to 2003 the executive director of the Adult Literacy Resource Institute at the University of Massachusetts Boston, and since 2003 has been president of Newsome Associates, an education consulting firm in Boston. He is the moderator of Technology and Learning, a U.S. Department of Education-sponsored LINCS national online adult basic skills community of practice; he is also a partner in the EdTech Center at World Education, Inc.*

DR. JENIFER B. VANEK *works as an adjunct instructor at the University of Minnesota, College of Education and Human Development. In her consulting work she serves as the director of the IDEAL Consortium, a project of the EdTech Center at World Education, Inc., and the digital literacy and education subject-matter expert for the Northstar Digital Literacy Assessment project of the Minnesota Literacy Council.*

New Directions for Adult and Continuing Education • DOI: 10.1002/ace

This chapter describes documented and undocumented immigrant populations in the United States. It discusses salient factors influencing their status as immigrants as well as adult education services available to them through publicly funded programs, social units, and community centers, especially churches and libraries.

Immigrants to the United States and Adult Education Services

Clarena Larrotta

Undeniably, the United States is a country made up of immigrants. Immigrants have been coming here to make this country their home since before the 15th century when Europeans set their eyes on the New World. Immigration to the United States has not always been regulated by law. It was not until 1819 when the first significant federal immigration law required ship captains to provide customs officials with a list of immigrants that described where they came from, where they were going, and their sex, age, and occupation (Annenberg Classroom, 2017). Social and political factors as well as the economic divides they face in their home countries reflect three different ways immigrants enter the country: "Regular immigration channels, refugees/asylees, and without legal authorization" (Rumbaut & Komaie, 2010, p. 43). Those who enter through either regular immigration channels or as refugees/asylees are termed "documented," whereas those who enter without legal authorization are "undocumented." These classifications can determine both the types of adult education services that immigrants need and the adult education programs available to them. Research and data on adult education services provided to documented immigrants are prolific. These populations are easily accounted for in the literature and educational services designed to meet their needs have clearly identifiable funding sources. However, there is a paucity of research on adult education services for undocumented adults.

This chapter describes salient factors influencing documented and undocumented immigrants as well as adult education services available to them through publicly funded programs, social units, and community centers (e.g., churches, libraries, parks, museums, and health and business institutions). Depending on their legal status, immigrants receive different treatment and

NEW DIRECTIONS FOR ADULT AND CONTINUING EDUCATION, no. 155, Fall 2017 © 2017 Wiley Periodicals, Inc.
Published online in Wiley Online Library (wileyonlinelibrary.com) • DOI: 10.1002/ace.20241

different services. The way they enter the country also determines the length of time they receive economic assistance and adult education services such as language classes and financial literacy instruction. Because federally funded services can often fall short in meeting the wide range of immigrant education needs, serving immigrants through nongovernmental agencies is crucial in order to reach both documented and undocumented immigrants. However, they frequently lack adequate funding and government support, which makes these agencies unstable and unable to keep up with this demand. This issue is highlighted as immigration numbers continue to grow, the need for services increases, and immigration laws become more unforgiving.

Adult Basic Education

The types of federally funded instructional services available to adults lacking literacy, numeracy, or English language skills needed to fully participate in work, family, and community include adult basic education, adult secondary education, and English as a second language programs (National Reporting System [NRS] for Adult Education, 2015). English as a second language (ESL) programs are intended to help adults with limited English language proficiency achieve competence for employment and other social interactions (NRS, 2015). Without English proficiency, immigrants are often locked into low-wage jobs, blocked from acquiring new skills and new jobs, denied equal access to health and other services, and shut off from contact with the larger society (American Immigrant Policy Portal, 2017).

To provide some context to the issue of how adult ESL programs are funded federally, a brief review of the history of adult basic education (ABE) is needed. In 1964, ABE first received federal funds as Title IIB of the Economic Opportunity Act, authorized through the Office of Economic Opportunity but administered by the U.S. Office of Education. The 1991 National Literacy Act (NLA) significantly expanded the scope and funding for federal adult education programs. In 1998, the Adult Education and Family Literacy Act under Title II of the Workforce Investment Act (WIA) replaced the NLA. Recently, in 2015, the Workforce Innovation and Opportunity Act (WIOA) replaced WIA and will be in effect until 2020. WIOA seeks to better align the workforce system with education and economic development to create a collective response to economic and labor market challenges. Those who are eligible to participate in WIOA-funded programs must meet the statute's definition of *adult, dislocated worker or displaced homemaker*, and must provide proof of U.S. Citizenship or Legal Alien status and Selective Service Registration (for males born on or after January 1, 1960), a social security number, and be at least 16 years old. Adult education for immigrants is also funded through WIOA; however, eligibility requirements clearly create barriers for participation. Undocumented immigrants cannot provide evidence of legal status or a social security number.

New Directions for Adult and Continuing Education • DOI: 10.1002/ace

Documented Immigrants

The category *documented immigrants* includes all persons who were granted lawful permanent residence, were granted asylum, were admitted as refugees, or arrived as nonimmigrant residents such as students and temporary workers (Baker & Rytina, 2013). In 2013, California, Texas, Florida, New York, and Illinois were the five largest recipients of documented immigrants.

Asylees and refugees are a subset of documented immigrants; yet, establishing the distinction between these two groups is crucial. The difference lies in where the person is located when making an application for immigration to the United States. Asylum status designates those persons who are *already* within the country or at a U.S. port of entry when they apply for legal status. Refugee status designates persons who are located outside of the United States as well as outside of their native countries at the time of their application. Zong and Batalova (2015) described refugees and asylees as individuals who are unable or unwilling to return to their countries of origin because of war; are the victims of persecution on the basis of their race, religion, membership in a group, or political opinion; or have been forced to abort a pregnancy, undergone forced sterilization, or suffered coercive population control.

In 2015, 70,000 refugees entered the country followed by 85,000 in 2016. According to the Worldwide Refugee Admissions Processing System, the top 10 refugee origin countries of those entering the United States in 2015 were Burma (26%), Iraq (18%), Somalia (12%), Congo (11%), Bhutan (8%), Iran (4%), and Syria, Eritrea, Sudan, and Cuba (2% each). However, this pattern changed in 2016 with nearly half of U.S. refugees coming from Congo, Syria, Somalia, and Burma. Specifically, Syria (15%) contributed larger refugee numbers than usual (Connor, 2016).

Because of their legal status, documented immigrants have available a variety of resources and services designed to ease their transition into U.S. culture and the economy. They have the opportunity and supports in place to help move them toward integration and self-sufficiency; this is a key goal of adult education programs that serve this population. However, in the case of refugee/asylees, these services have an expiration date and are not comprehensive enough to cover educational needs related to why and how they entered the country.

The U.S. Department of Health and Human Services Office of Refugee Resettlement provides time-limited cash and medical assistance to new arrivals, as well as funding for case management services, English language classes, job readiness, and employment services to support a successful transition to attaining self-sufficiency. It supports additional programs, beyond the first 8 months post arrival, including microenterprise development, ethnic community self-help, and agricultural partnerships. However, the duration of these services is limited because of the growing number of refugees and inadequate infrastructure.

In summary, the challenges that adult documented immigrants face are related to the relatively short period of time they are allowed to stay enrolled in adult education programs, the growing demand for these services, and limited funding. For example, only 12% of WIOA funds have been specifically designated for ESL/civics; yet, ESL students comprise over 40% of WIOA Title II enrollments (Murphy, 2014). Programs are held accountable by WIOA for economic and educational outcomes as well as progress in English language acquisition and civics education (Murphy, 2014, p. 4). WIOA's goal is to help adults transition (as soon as possible) into the workforce and economic self-sufficiency. Under this provision, other education services such as courses on parenting, nutrition, acculturation, and extended ESL education and job readiness are not available. These, and other skills, are services that immigrant adults need to receive for longer periods of time to successfully adapt to living in the United States.

Undocumented Immigrants

The U.S. Department of Homeland Security defines *undocumented immigrants* as all foreign-born noncitizens who are not legal residents. Undocumented immigrants "either entered the country without inspection or were admitted temporarily and stayed past the date they were required to leave" (Hoefer, Rytina, & Baker, 2011, p. 1). It is estimated that 300,000 to 500,000 undocumented immigrants enter the U.S. economy each year; some return to their country and others are deported (Briggs, 2012, p. 957). In 2013 an estimated 11.3 million undocumented immigrants were living in the United States (Passel, Cohn, Krogstad, & Gonzales-Barrera, 2014). The median length of U.S. residency was nearly 13 years; at least 20% had lived in the United States for more than 20 years (Passel et al. 2014). They have made it their home and are not planning to leave unless they are deported.

The United States lacks a federal policy for naturalization and citizenship of long-term undocumented residents. On the contrary, every year additional restrictive policies are created to punish and stigmatize undocumented persons and limit opportunities to access education and social services. We lack a coherent immigrant integration policy (e.g., cultural, workforce, legal integration); often community-based entities fill in the gaps to address the education and training needs of immigrant adults. Yet, regardless of legal status, immigrants who can understand English and use literacy and numeracy to participate in jobs, their communities, and their children's education are more likely to benefit society than cost it. Research has shown that literacy and numeracy skills are correlated with a wide range of positive outcomes (Organisation for Economic Cooperation and Development, 2013); once immigrants are in the country, regardless of legal status, it is to our advantage to provide educational services for them.

In the past, as a way to counteract the persecution and harassment that undocumented immigrants experience, some states created a number of sanctuary jurisdictions or immigrant friendly communities (Wrigley, 2012, p. 28). Citing Vaughan (2016), the Center for Immigration Studies' webpage stated that some opposed sanctuary jurisdictions because they have laws or practices that obstruct immigration enforcement and shield criminals from Immigration and Customs Enforcement (ICE; http://cis.org/Sanctuary-Cities-Map). Political and legal grounds for sanctuary continue to decrease, and in many jurisdictions there have never been any such protections. Needless to say, this fractured approach toward undocumented immigrants will continue to affect their access to adult education services. Although an instructional capacity could potentially be built up to meet the flow of these adults into the adult education system, nobody really knows how many undocumented immigrants will need ESL/civics instruction in the next 10 years. This makes it difficult to set realistic annual service goals for them (Murphy, 2014, pp. 1–2). Given current eligibility requirements, undocumented immigrants will always be at a disadvantage when seeking education and employment regardless of other immigration policy shifts.

Unfortunately, under the Trump Administration, the conditions for undocumented immigrants are rapidly changing for the worse; they are likely to experience increasing persecution and discrimination. Not only might opportunities for undocumented immigrants to enroll in adult education programs become slimmer (as more regulations and documentation requirements are put into place to receive federal funding), increased fear might make it far less likely that those who could benefit from adult education would even try to.

Adult Education Services for Immigrants

To document adult education services, evaluate federally funded adult education programs, and better understand the skills of the participants enrolled in these programs, the U.S. Department of Education funded the Adult Education Program Survey in 2007. More than 1,200 adult education programs participated in this survey; these programs included five groups: Local Education Agencies (LEAs, 54%), community-based organizations (CBOs, 24%), community colleges (17%), correctional institutions (2%), and combination providers (3%) (Tamassia, Lennon, Yamamoto, & Kirsch, 2007, p. 23). LEAs and CBOs provide valuable information and serve as a bridge to services that undocumented immigrants would not otherwise know about. It is likely that a considerable percentage of adult immigrants enroll to receive adult education services, ESL, and literacy education through both LEAs and CBOs. However, there is little reported in the literature about this.

Social service agencies, community centers, and especially churches and libraries also provide adult education services for immigrants. Religious agencies have sponsored refugees since the 1950s and have played a leading role in arranging and implementing immigrant resettlement, advocating for human rights, cultivating growth of cultural tolerance, and maintaining a basic doctrine of nondiscrimination (Chiba, 2014, p. 10). These are important practices given the current state of strict and harsh immigration policies endorsed by President Trump and implemented by the U.S. Immigration and Customs Enforcement (ICE) agency. The policies and leadership of this new administration have heightened anti-immigration sentiments and discriminatory practices against immigrants that had grown relatively dormant in most regions. In contrast, religious institutions continue to model a practice of multiculturalism and acceptance and provide additional services to assist immigrants in acculturation and healing processes as they deal with culture shock and issues caused by immigration trauma.

An example of a successful church-sponsored educational initiative for immigrants is the establishment of community gardens. Hartwig and Mason (2016) reported that these gardens serve as a meaningful educational intervention for refugees, and immigrants in general, adjusting to life in the United States or coping with past traumas. They found that refugees received physical and emotional benefits from gardening; for those who worked in agriculture before immigrating it built a comforting connection between their new lives and their former selves. In addition, the therapeutic and shared communal space of the garden served as a comfortable location for health and social support interventions from English language classes to chronic disease prevention trainings (Hartwig & Mason, 2016). In other words, these community gardens provided the space for immigrants to make friends, interact with a variety of people and services, practice English, gain a sense of belonging, and learn about the local culture and agriculture practices.

A recent ethnographic study conducted by Chao and Mantero (2014) reported on the ways in which Latino and Asian immigrant parents learning English through two different church-based ESL programs benefitted. Their data suggest that family literacy and home language practices were positively affected. Chao and Mantero concluded that the programs were empowering experiences that promoted ESL learning while building on their funds of knowledge and contributed to advancing family literacy practices in English. This study presented church-based ESL programs as social mediators situating immigrants within U.S. communities, empowering their families' literacies, accessing communities of power, and having a voice in the larger society (Chao & Mantero, 2014, pp. 108–109).

Likewise, libraries play an important role in providing adult education opportunities for immigrants. Pete (2016) found that learners participating in a library-sponsored ESL program reported improved English communication skills in the workplace, conversation skills, and grammar; they were able to do banking and shopping without fear and felt greater confidence and more independence and experienced joy when socializing in English. Another related report found that library staff members refer immigrants to local agencies and organizations, provide information on community services, and help them integrate into their communities (U.S. Citizenship and Immigration Services, Office of Citizenship, 2006). These findings align well with current research describing the evolution of libraries as community development centers focusing on social empowerment, economic development, and lifelong learning (Shrestha & Krolak, 2015).

The demand for publicly funded adult education keeps growing as does the number of immigrants entering the country; however, the funding for adult education programs remains the same or decreases depending on the nation's immigration policies and how the different states are applying them. The work that religious groups and libraries are doing to support the efforts of publicly funded adult education is timely and crucial. Publicly funded programs are not enough for serving the growing need for immigrant education services. At present, religious groups and other social service agencies take up much of the slack and continue to play an important role in advocating for the compassionate integration of immigrants to U.S. society, promoting human rights, and providing needed support services and education. Likewise, libraries have shifted from being just repositories of books and information to becoming proactive service providers that promote community development and assist people seeking to improve their quality of life (Shrestha & Krolak, 2015, p. 403). The role of libraries in helping adult immigrants to further develop ESL proficiency is of critical importance.

Conclusion

Immigrants to the United States are participating in adult education and family education initiatives in large numbers across the country. Like documented immigrants, undocumented immigrants also participate in classes related to ESL, nutrition, parenting, immigration issues, and other informal education opportunities available through local community-based education initiatives. By 2030, nearly one in five U.S. workers will be an immigrant (Myers, Levy, & Pitkin, 2013); however, many questions remain about the adult education infrastructure and successful integration of documented and undocumented immigrants. Although there is a lack of research on the participation of undocumented immigrants in adult education, it seems likely that they are participating. Research is needed to address many questions that could help serve them better. For example, what factors have contributed to their transition into U.S. life? How have they coped with the trauma of illegal immigration? How will the country and the education system deal with the large number of undocumented children currently transitioning to adulthood? What role will adult education programs play in helping them achieve social and economic integration? These are important questions to consider when planning publicly funded adult education efforts.

In the meantime, social service agencies and community centers such as libraries, parks, museums, health institutions, business organizations, and churches continue to offer education services to all types of immigrants, playing an important role of filling in where federally funded programs leave gaps. Even though these providers generally have the freedom to serve documented and undocumented immigrants, it is risky to depend so heavily on them given that they do so without adequate support. They are offering a variety of needed services such as community gardening, wellness and nutrition, parenting, ESL/literacy, financial literacy, and computer classes. They are also directly and indirectly helping immigrants cope with different types of trauma related to their immigration status. They offer important contexts for research and practice that could inform government-funded programs. However, they do so under unstable and underresourced conditions. The federal government could take greater responsibility, revise immigration policy, and lead the way in sustained efforts to effectively integrate immigrants.

Policymakers and publicly funded adult education providers need to keep in mind that as immigrants strive to integrate into the U.S. workforce, it is in our best interest to help them build on and develop their current education and work skills/experience. Adult education programs can provide opportunities for them to acquire additional education and training that will contribute to their personal prosperity and that of the country. Adult education programs should evolve with and reflect the country's demographics; this means meeting the needs of all adult learners regardless of their immigration status. Despite repressive and punitive policies that have encouraged recent raids performed by ICE throughout the country and targeted community adult education centers, adult educators should continue in service to the foundational goal of the field—to promote adult learning and development, knowledge, and lifelong learning. Many immigrants have vital educational needs; addressing them not only helps them, it benefits us all.

References

American Immigrant Policy Portal. (2017). *Adult education and workforce training abstracts*. Retrieved from http://www.usdiversitydynamics.com/nj/id8.html

Annenberg Classroom. (2017). Immigration timeline. Retrieved from http://www.annenbergclassroom.org/files/documents/immigration.pdf

Baker, B., & Rytina, N. (2013). *Estimates of the unauthorized immigrant populations residing in the United States: January 2012*. Washington, DC: U.S. Department of Homeland Security, Office of Immigration Statistics. Retrieved from https://www.dhs.gov/sites/default/files/publications/ois_ill_pe_2012_2.pdf

Briggs, V. M., Jr. (2012). The elusive goal: The quest for a credible immigration policy. *Journal of Policy Analysis and Management, 31*(4), 956–963.

Chao, X., & Mantero, M. (2014). Church-based ESL adult programs: Social mediators for empowering "family literacy ecology communities." *Journal of Literacy Research, 46*(1), 90–114. https://doi.org/10.1177/1086296X14524588

Chiba, H. (2014). The role of Protestant church in the US refugee resettlement program during the early cold war era: The Methodist case. *Exchange, 43*, 9–28.

Connor, P. (2016). *U.S. admits record number of Muslim refugees in 2016*. Washington, DC: Pew Research Center. Retrieved from http://www.pewresearch.org/fact-tank/2016/10/05/u-s-admits-record-number-of-muslim-refugees-in-2016/

Hartwig, K. A., & Mason, M. (2016). Community gardens for refugee and immigrant communities as a means of health promotion. *Journal of Community Health, 41*, 1153–1159.

Hoefer, M., Rytina, N., & Baker, B. C. (2011). *Estimates of the unauthorized immigrant population residing in the United States: January 2010*. Washington, DC: U.S.

New Directions for Adult and Continuing Education • DOI: 10.1002/ace

Department of Homeland Security, Office of Immigration Statistics. Retrieved from https://www.dhs.gov/xlibrary/assets/statistics/publications/ois_ill_pe_2010.pdf

Murphy, G. (with Spangenberg, G.). (2014). *Size & flow: Adult education issues in the Senate immigration bill*. New York, NY: Council for Advancement of Adult Literacy.

Myers, D., Levy, S., & Pitkin, J. (2013). *The contributions of immigrants and their children to the American workforce and jobs of the future*. Washington, DC: Center for American Progress.

National Reporting System for Adult Education. (2015). *Measures and methods for the National Reporting System for adult education—Implementation guidelines*. Washington, DC: U.S. Department of Education, Division of Adult Education and Literacy, Office of Vocational and Adult Education.

Organisation for Economic Cooperation and Development. (2013). *Skilled for life? Key findings from the survey of adult skills*. Paris: Author. Retrieved from http://www.oecd.org/skills/piaac/SkillsOutlook_2013_ebook.pdf

Passel, J. S., Cohn, D., Krogstad, J. M., & Gonzalez-Barrera, A. (2014). *As growth stalls, unauthorized immigrant population becomes more settled*. Washington, DC: Pew Research Center. Retrieved from http://www.pewhispanic.org/2014/09/03/as-growth-stalls-unauthorized-immigrant-population-becomes-more-settled/

Pete, J. K. (2016). A library's role in the success of adult English learners. *MPAEA Journal of Adult Education, 45*(1), 1–8.

Rumbaut, R. G., & Komaie, G. (2010). Immigration and adult transitions. *Future of Children, 20*(1), 43–66.

Shrestha, S., & Krolak, L. (2015). The potential of community libraries in supporting literate environments and sustaining literacy skills. *International Review of Education, 61*(3), 399–418. https://doi.org/10.1007/s11159-014-9462-9

Tamassia, C., Lennon, M., Yamamoto, K., & Kirsch, I. (2007). *Adult education in America: A first look at results from the adult education program and learner surveys*. Princeton, NJ: Educational Testing Service.

U.S. Citizenship and Immigration Services, Office of Citizenship. (2006). *Library services for immigrants: A report on current practices*. Washington, DC: Author. Retrieved from https://www.uscis.gov/sites/default/files/USCIS/Office%20of%20Citizenship/Citizenship%20Resource%20Center%20Site/Publications/G-1112.pdf

Vaughan, J. (2016, August 31). CIS–Sanctuary cities continue to obstruct enforcement, threaten public safety. Retrieved from http://www.helpsavemaryland.org/?p=2768

Wrigley, H. S. (2012). Dimensions of immigrant integration and civic engagement: Issues and exemplary programs. In L. Muñoz & H. G. Wrigley (Eds.), *New Directions for Adult and Continuing Education: No. 135. Adult Civic Engagement in Adult Learning* (pp. 25–32). San Francisco, CA: Jossey-Bass.

Zong, J., & Batalova, J. (2015). *Refugees and asylees in the United States*. Washington, DC: Migration Policy Institute. Retrieved from http://www.migrationpolicy.org/article/refugees-and-asylees-united-states

CLARENA LARROTTA is an associate professor at Texas State University. She teaches in the Adult, Professional, and Community Education Programs.

7

This chapter offers an update on efforts to provide all adult basic education teachers with access to high-quality professional development.

Professional Development and Professionalization in the Field of Adult Basic Education

Cristine Smith

An interesting phenomenon occurred in Massachusetts in 1988 and 1989. Through an initiative from Governor Michael Dukakis, the Commonwealth of Massachusetts conducted a multiyear project, the Commonwealth Literacy Corps (CLC), to train volunteer tutors to work with adult learners inside and outside of their adult basic education (ABE) program classrooms. The initiative involved developing and delivering a 15-hour training for tutors who would work with adult basic education or English for Speakers of other Languages (ESOL) learners. After several years of conducting training for volunteers, the CLC staff began to hear rumblings from ABE teachers[1] who had volunteer tutors working with them as aides in their classrooms; it seemed the teachers were frustrated that the tutors had more knowledge and skills (because of the 15-hour training they had attended) than they did. This was understandable, because—at that time—the only training that Massachusetts ABE teachers received were single workshops offered by one paid consultant.

In 1990, as a result of this and other factors, Massachusetts initiated the System for Adult Basic Education Support (SABES), a statewide ABE professional development system. It offered a wide range of regional workshops, institutes, and technical assistance. Although many ABE teachers still received no preservice training, at least there was a relatively well-funded system to provide ongoing, inservice professional development—at that time, called "staff development"—to all teachers in the state.

Between 1990 and 2006, the delivery of adult basic education professional development advanced considerably across the country. For example, states developed systems for professional development built on evidence-based practice and professional wisdom (Belzer, Drennon, & Smith, 2001). The National Literacy Act 1991 and the Workforce Investment Act of 1998 (federal funding authorizations for the field) provided state and national

NEW DIRECTIONS FOR ADULT AND CONTINUING EDUCATION, no. 155, Fall 2017 © 2017 Wiley Periodicals, Inc.
Published online in Wiley Online Library (wileyonlinelibrary.com) • DOI: 10.1002/ace.20242

leadership with funding for professional development, and state ABE directors promoted professional development through their own national associations. The National Center for the Study of Adult Literacy (NCSALL) conducted research on professional development (Smith, Hofer, Gillespie, Solomon, & Rowe, 2003) and developed multiple models for professional development—study circles, workshops, practitioner research—through which research could reach ABE teachers and program directors with evidence about how to improve the quality of instruction for adult learners. This chapter updates the progress and trends in professional development over the past 10 years in the adult basic education field by describing implications of recent legislation on professional development policy and practice, professional development for teachers who work with specific adult learner populations, and an increased emphasis on the professionalization of the field.

Policy Context for Professional Development: A Focus on Quality

From 1998 to 2014, federal funding and policy for adult literacy and basic education had been authorized under the Workforce Investment Act (WIA). Congress reauthorized and renamed it in 2014; it is now known as the Workforce Innovation and Opportunity Act (WIOA) (U.S. Congress, 2014). This new statute heightens attention on providing high-quality professional development to teachers toward the goal of improving adult learner outcomes. For example, the Office of Career, Technical, and Adult Education (OCTAE), the U.S. Department of Education unit that oversees adult basic and literacy education, can now offer direct technical assistance to teachers "related to professional development activities" (WIOA Sec 242 (c)1(A)) or fund other organizations to develop "high-quality professional development activities for eligible providers," e.g., programs offering services (WIOA Sec 242 (c)2(C)vi). Under WIOA, there is also a new emphasis on professional development that will help ABE teachers integrate technology into instruction.

Other policies originally established under WIA continue under WIOA. For example, the new act has language emphasizing the need for professional development focused on evidence-based practice, defined as "the development and dissemination of instructional and programmatic practices based on the most rigorous or scientifically valid research available and appropriate, in reading, writing, speaking, mathematics, English language acquisition programs, distance education, and staff training" (WIOA Sec 223 (a)1(C)i). In addition, every state agency responsible for overseeing adult basic and literacy education continues to receive a "leadership" grant from the federal government; this allows them to use up to 12.5% of the state's WIOA allocation for leadership activities. Under WIA, states used this leadership funding for a wide range of activities, including professional development, research, and support for the rollout of new initiatives. However, WIOA now provides guidance for using those state funds specifically to promote high-quality professional

New Directions for Adult and Continuing Education • DOI: 10.1002/ace

development (PD) to improve teaching. WIOA's specific references to the type and quality of professional development indicate a growing realization among policymakers that improving learner outcomes depends, at least in part, on ABE teachers participating in continuous, effective professional learning opportunities. Moreover, WIOA includes language tying state funding to teacher quality and professional development. Eligible providers receive WIOA funds based on, among other criteria, "whether the eligible provider's activities are delivered by well-trained instructors, counselors, and administrators who meet any minimum qualifications established by the State, where applicable, and who have access to high quality professional development, including through electronic means" (WIOA Sec 231 (e)5(9)).

Definition of and Structures for High-Quality Professional Development

Establishing expectations for "high-quality" professional development begs the question of how this is defined. Enough research has been done about effective, evidence-based PD—both in K–12 (Hattie, 2009; Timperley, Wilson, Barrar, & Fung, 2007) and in adult basic education (Smith, et al., 2003)—that professional developers, and now policymakers, cannot ignore the fact that one-off, single-session workshops, a staple in settings such as conferences, are the least effective professional development model. Instead, effective professional development takes place over a longer span of time. This gives teachers more opportunities to reflect on, pose questions about, and critique their current beliefs and practices, to learn new concepts and skills, and to try out and then get feedback on new practices. It also offers opportunities for job-embedded teacher communities of practice to collaborate around identifying and solving problems of practice and for exposing teachers to outside information from research and experts as a way to learn about and become proficient at implementing new instructional approaches that can improve learner outcomes (Hattie, 2009; Smith & Gillespie, 2007; Timperley et al., 2007). Specifically, Hattie's massive review of research on professional development in 2009 indicates that the four professional learning activities most supportive of improved student learning were (a) observation of actual classroom instruction; (b) microteaching (short mini-lessons teachers deliver to peers or in real classrooms, with observation and feedback); (c) use of video to provide teachers with feedback about teaching; and (d) teaching practice where teachers are guided to actively reflect on and evaluate the effect of their teaching on students' learning. In addition, Timperley et al. (2007), assessing over 70 studies on the connection between professional development and learner outcomes, found that teacher communities of practice were necessary but not sufficient for teacher change and that input from external experts added to teachers' effectiveness and improved learner outcomes. It is worth noting that all of these prescriptions for high-quality professional development require policies at the national and state level that fund and structure professional development and learning opportunities for adult basic education teachers at a level far beyond what has been available to date.

In alignment with efforts from researchers, professional developers, and policymakers to make effective PD the primary mechanism for improving the quality of instruction in the field, OCTAE sponsored an effort in 2013, titled Promoting Teacher Effectiveness in Adult Education, which produced a set of teacher competencies, a self-assessment guide for teachers, and an anno- tated bibliography of research on professional development. Recognizing that, unlike K–12 teachers, ABE teachers seldom receive preservice training before they begin teaching adults, an additional product of the Teacher Effectiveness project was to develop guidelines and a toolkit for teacher induction to support beginning teachers during their early years in the field (American Institutes for Research, 2015).

During the past 10 years, professional development for ABE practition- ers has become more centralized. In 2010, building on the LINCS electronic information and resource clearinghouse started by the National Institute for Literacy, the Office of Vocational and Adult Education (the U.S. Department of Education unit overseeing ABE and later to become OCTAE) supplemented LINCS through four federally funded regional PD centers that offered both on- line and face-to-face PD to augment LINCS' virtual resources. Then, starting in 2016, OCTAE replaced the regional centers with a national LINCS PD Center to:

> assist states to leverage the many resources and capabilities in the LINCS sys- tem to meet two WIOA requirements for state leadership activities [including] online courses, online Community of Practice (COP) platform, in-person train- ing packages, talent pools, tools and resources … [through] a tiered menu of services to meet the varied needs and to allow for and support localization of the offerings. This menu will provide tiers and options of services to assist with PD program establishment or operation and with dissemination of LINCS' PD resources and learning experiences. (Office of Career, Technical, and Adult Ed- ucation, 2016)

Finally, the availability of online and blended (online plus face-to-face) professional development has exploded, supported by LINCS and by states such as California (CalPRO), through the LINCS Regional PD Centers, and through nonprofit agencies such as World Education, ProLiteracy, and the Center for Literacy, Education and Employment (CLEE). From free webinars to for-fee courses, ABE teachers now have many more opportunities to access professional development. It is unclear whether and to what extent such virtual professional development can include the features of high-quality, evidence- based professional development, but for a field where part-time teachers can be isolated in their programs, or programs can be isolated in their states, the accessibility of online PD is a welcome turn of events. It remains to be seen how they affect teachers' practices and adult learner outcomes.

New Directions for Adult and Continuing Education • DOI: 10.1002/ace

The question remains whether national initiatives such as these are integrated into state PD systems and, if they are integrated, how states will also afford to offer locally based and job-embedded professional development. A comprehensive state PD system should offer a range of activities, based on the types of knowledge teachers need during their careers (Smith, 2010). Specifically, a system needs to help teachers access professional development that provides different types of knowledge: *knowing about* new research and instructional strategies, *knowing that* new strategies are effective, *knowing how* to implement new and evidence-based strategies, and *knowing whether and why* such strategies will work and for which learners. Another consideration for PD providers when planning high-quality PD is how to offer professional development content and formats that fit the different experiences, current knowledge, and beliefs of adult basic education teachers (Hattie, 2009). Just as learners benefit from differentiated instruction, PD systems would ideally offer "differentiated PD."

The need for both diverse and targeted PD argues for a wide range of information-sharing resources in a PD system using multiple platforms and media, including newsletters, blogs, listservs, online webinars, face-to-face or blended multisession workshops, on-site teacher study groups, and action research. Ideally, an array of PD choices would allow new, experienced, part-time and full-time teachers to gain the knowledge and skills they need in a "package" that works for them. There is likely little opportunity to do anything other than surmise the benefits of such a plethora of PD opportunities due to scarce resources, even under legislation that prioritizes high-quality PD.

Professional Development for Teachers of Specific Adult Learner Populations

Although the Office of Vocational and Adult Education (OVAE) previously supported extensive professional development initiatives aimed at improving the teaching of basic skills, such as the Student Achievement in Reading (STAR) professional development program designed to improve reading instruction, and the Teaching Excellence in Adult Literacy (TEAL) program PD for teaching writing, other initiatives have the goal of better preparing adult basic education teachers to work with specific populations of learners. For example, Learning to Achieve is a multimodal, multimodule professional development program, implemented through the LINCS Regional PD Centers, that aims to help teachers better serve adult learners with learning disabilities. The United States Citizenship and Immigration Services (USCIS) has developed extensive resources for ABE programs and teachers that offer English-language and citizenship education services to adults, including a set of content standards for citizenship education, a guidebook on elements of program quality for ESOL/citizenship education programs, lesson plans for adult citizenship education instructors, and online courses through English Language

Learner University (ELL-U), a training and professional development network for ESOL teachers.

Perhaps the most significant focus in the past decade has been the exponential growth in professional development around career and college readiness. In line with the increasing emphasis on adult learner transition to, persistence in, and successful completion of postsecondary education, as well as the federal focus on workforce development, ABE teachers can access almost unlimited information and training about how to structure instruction to help adult learners move into jobs and further education. State, national, and foundation funding have produced a bounty of resources for organizing, funding, improving, and evaluating career and college readiness programs, and these resources are continuing to make their way into PD opportunities at all levels.

Professionalization of the Field

Shanahan, Meehan, and Mogge (1994) define *professionalization* as:

> the movement of any field towards some standards of educational preparation and competency. The term professionalization indicates a direct attempt to (a) use education or training to improve the quality of practice, (b) standardize professional responses, (c) better define a collection of persons as representing a field of endeavor, and (d) enhance communication within that field. (p. 1)

Multiple aspects of the field of adult basic education contribute to the idea that teachers of adult learners are not "real" professionals, in contrast to their counterparts in K–12 and higher education. These aspects include the part-time nature of employment for the majority of ABE teachers; the historical dependence upon minimally trained volunteers to teach adult learners, especially for those at the lowest reading levels; the funding structure for adult education, which depends largely on unstable, year-to-year government appropriations and grant funding rather than property taxes or tuition that is virtually guaranteed over time, thus allowing instructors in schools and colleges to acquire tenure based on performance; the multitude of ABE providers, from school districts to private organizations to churches to volunteer organizations, which often operate in temporary and shared space; and the lack of professional certification or licensure, or even preservice training, required by states and programs before teachers step into an adult education classroom.

The primary component of a professional field is certification or licensure of its workers, as exemplified by professional fields such as medicine, law, accounting, and even early childhood educators, to name a few. Certification or licensure requires four elements: (a) a set of competencies or standards that define what professionals should know and be able to do, (b) availability of professional education opportunities to help workers gain those competencies, (c) a mechanism for testing or assuring that workers meet the standards, and (d) incentives that make getting a certification attractive to teachers (Smith &

New Directions for Adult and Continuing Education • DOI: 10.1002/ace

Gomez, 2011). Requirements for entry and maintaining a position in the field would serve as one incentive, and rewards in the form of stable employment or higher salaries for teachers would be another.

Although the vast majority of ABE teachers are well credentialed, with either a bachelor's or a master's degree (Cronen, Yin, & Condelli, 2015; Smith & Hofer, 2003, their degrees are in a wide variety of disciplines; professionalization through training and certification specifically as ABE instructors is still lacking in most states. Although adult basic education teachers who are employed by local educational authorities (LEAs, e.g., school districts) are typically required to have at least K–12 certification, teachers in other types of programs generally are not.

Since 2006, there has been increasing dialogue in the field about whether lack of professionalization of the workforce contributes to ABE being underfunded and treated as a "second-class" cousin to the P–16 education systems. The National Center for the Study of Adult Learning and Literacy commissioned an article on the landscape of certification and professionalization for the adult basic education field, which indicated the contentious nature of the issue. There is a division between those who valued certification and those who feel that it would act as a "gatekeeper" that would prevent good teachers from entering or staying in the field because getting a certificate would be too onerous in cost, time, and effort (Sabatini, Ginsburg & Russell, 2002). Almost 10 years later, the Council for the Advancement of Adult Literacy (CAAL) sponsored research, an online survey, and a meeting of adult education experts and policymakers leading to two reports on adult education certification (Chisman, 2011; Smith & Gomez, 2011). These reports provide a backdrop on discussions about the connection between certification and teacher quality and the pros, cons, and challenges of setting up an adult education certification system and a suggested path forward. In 2012, following the publication of these reports, the McGraw-Hill Research Foundation, working with the Commission for Adult Basic Education (COABE) and the National Adult Education Professional Development Consortium (NAEPDC), funded the development of a report (Hess, McLendon, Moore, & Rosin, 2012) about the need for a national adult education teacher credential, laying out an implementation plan that starts with the creation of an ABE mathematics teacher credential. It is unclear, at the time of this writing, whether and how that initiative is moving forward.

In recent years, the federal government has endeavored to define and support statewide processes for professionalizing the field. Building on the work that the 1999 Pro-Net project, TESOL, and the Association of Adult Literacy Professional Developers (AALPD) had done to create a framework for what teachers are expected to know and be able to do as instructors, the OVAE-funded project on teacher effectiveness produced a set of competencies, indicators, self-assessment, and online courses for ABE teachers that could be used as the foundation for a national or state-level certification.

Some states have progressed in making voluntary certification available to ABE teachers. For example, in 2004, Massachusetts established a voluntary licensure process—Adult Basic Education License—valid for 5 years and renewable every 5 years, with four different routes to certification depending on a teacher's years of experience in the field. Built on 29 specific standards, developed by SABES with funding from the state department of education, the licensure process requires teachers to complete a performance assessment and a teaching demonstration, and attain passing scores on a Communication and Literacy Skills Test and an ABE Subject Matter Knowledge Test, specifically developed for this teacher license.

Other states have also been experimenting with credentialing models, voluntary or required, that range from participating in formal graduate courses—either face to face or online—to providing evidence of teacher effectiveness. Virginia created an online credentialing program through Virginia Commonwealth University in which teachers take six three-credit courses online to qualify. Minnesota's licensure program is based on graduate classes at the University of Minnesota, including 12 credit hours for already-licensed K–12 teachers and 24 credits of coursework for adult education teachers with no previous licensure. Colorado has one of the few required credentials, the Adult Basic Education Authorization, which is now the "minimum professional standard for instructors in Colorado adult education programs that receive AEFLA [federal] funding" (Colorado Department of Education, 2014, p. 2). The certificate requires completion of four three-credit graduate courses related to teaching adults, as well as a portfolio documenting ABE employment history, training, and observations/evaluation. Also unusual is Nevada's Adult Basic Educator's Certificate of Performance, granted for 3 years and renewable, because it is based on evidence of the applying teacher's learners' successful persistence, skills, or further education and/or employment outcomes.

Also in 2004, Texas initiated a voluntary Adult Education Teacher Credential process, through the Education Initiative at the Texas State University, and commissioned a study of learner outcomes for adults studying with credentialed teachers as compared to noncredentialed teachers. Although only a small percentage of teachers had participated in the credential process by the time the study was done, preliminary findings indicated that learners participating in classes with credentialed teachers, as compared to those with noncredentialed teachers', made significantly greater gains on standardized tests of basic skills (Payne, Reardon, Janyssek, Lorenz, & Lampi, 2013). However, Texas State suspended the credential in 2013, pending a review by the Texas Workforce Commission.

Research on the relationship between certification and learner outcomes may be limited because relatively few adult basic education teachers have acquired credentials where it is voluntary. In Texas, for example, as of 2012, less than 2% of all teachers (Payne et al., 2013), and in Massachusetts, approximately 7% of adult basic education teachers have successfully completed

New Directions for Adult and Continuing Education • DOI: 10.1002/ace

the licensure process (World Education, 2016). It would also be difficult, if not impossible, to gauge whether such certification processes are indeed contributing to professionalization of the field in teachers', learners', or the public's eyes. However, it is clear that the issue of and progress toward certification and professionalization has received more attention at all levels in the past decade.

Conclusion

This review of projects, research, and initiatives to support adult basic education teachers' professional learning and to improve the quality of instruction indicates that teacher effectiveness, professional development, and professionalization have emerged as important issues in the field, in legislation, and in practice. With the assumption that investing in teachers' knowledge and skills would help adult learners be more likely to reach their goals, the new WIOA legislative mandate for high-quality professional development to increase teacher effectiveness signals a new and long-needed emphasis on the role and potential of professional development. However, there are several potential barriers to true progress in ensuring teachers' access to the best professional development. Writing at the start of a new administration, it is very unclear whether the funding and policy environment will be sufficient over the next 4 years to generate action in these areas. In addition, the increased focus on accountability that was ushered in by the No Child Left Behind Act in the early 1990s still envelopes attempts to improve quality in the adult basic education system. Finally, the reluctance or inability of policymakers to tackle the longstanding problem of low teacher salaries and poor working conditions means that new professional development initiatives are overlaid on the realities of teacher attrition in a field in which teachers piece together multiple part-time jobs, without benefits, in order to stay in the field. Research over the next 10 years should attempt to document the relationship between policies and provision of high-quality professional development and its relationship to teacher learning and change and, ultimately, to learner outcomes.

Notes

1. In this chapter, the phrase "adult basic education" refers to all adult education teachers who teach adults who want to improve literacy, numeracy, or English skills, or who are studying to obtain their high school equivalency.

References

American Institute for Research. (2015). *Teacher induction and a toolkit for adult educators.* Washington, DC: Author. Retrieved from https://lincs.ed.gov/publications/te/toolkit.pdf

Belzer, A., Drennon, C., & Smith, C. (2001). Building professional development systems in adult basic education: Lessons from the field. In J. Comings, B. Garner, & C. Smith (Eds.), *Review of adult learning and literacy* (Vol. 2, pp. 151–188). San Francisco, CA: Jossey-Bass.

Chisman, F. (2011). *Closing the gap: The challenge of certification and credentialing in adult education.* New York, NY: Council for Advancement of Adult Literacy.

Colorado Department of Education. (2014). *ABE authorization handbook, Section 1.2.* Retrieved from https://www.cde.state.co.us/cdeadult/11abeauth_14

Cronen, S., Yin, M., & Condelli, L. (2015). *Teachers of adult education and the students they serve: A snapshot from three states.* Washington, DC: American Institutes for Research.

Hattie, J. (2009). *Visible learning: A synthesis of meta-analyses relating to achievement.* New York, NY: Routledge.

Hess, M., McLendon, L., Moore, B., & Rosin, M. (2012). *Improving adult education teacher effectiveness: A call to action for a new credential.* New York, NY: McGraw-Hill Research Foundation.

Office of Career, Technical, and Adult Education. (2016). LINCS PD Center: A new model. Retrieved from https://sites.ed.gov/octae/2016/03/17/lincs-pd-center-a-new-model/

Payne, E. M., Reardon, R. F., Janysek, D. M., Lorenz, M., & Lampi, J. P. (2013). *Impact on student performance: Texas adult education teacher credential study preliminary results.* San Marcos, TX: Texas State University.

Sabatini, J.P., Ginsberg, L., & Russell, M. (2002). Professionalization and certification for teachers in adult basic education. Chapter 6. In J. Comings, B. Garner, & C. Smith (Eds.), *Annual Review of Adult Learning and Literacy*, Volume 3. San Francisco, CA: Jossey-Bass.

Shanahan, T., Meehan, M., & Mogge, S. (1994). *The professionalization of the teacher in adult literacy education.* Philadelphia, PA: National Center on Adult Literacy.

Smith, C. (2010). The great dilemma of improving teacher quality in adult learning and literacy. *Adult Basic Education and Literacy*, 4(2), 67–74.

Smith, C., & Gillespie, M. (2007). Research on professional development and teacher change: Implications for adult basic education. In J. Comings, B. Garner, & C. Smith (Eds.), *Review of adult learning and literacy* (Vol. 7, pp. 205–244). Mahwah, NJ: Lawrence Erlbaum Associates.

Smith, C., & Gomez, R. (2011). *Certifying adult education staff and faculty.* New York: Council for Advancement of Adult Literacy. Retrieved from http://www.caalusa.org/certteach.pdf

Smith, C. & Hofer, J. (2003). *The characteristics and concerns of adult basic education teachers (NCSALL Reports #26).* Boston, MA: National Center for the Study of Adult Learning and Literacy.

Smith, C., Hofer, J., Gillespie, M., Solomon, M., & Rowe, K. (2003). *How teachers change: A study of professional development in adult basic education (NCSALL Reports #25).* Boston, MA: National Center for the Study of Adult Learning and Literacy. Retrieved from http://www.ncsall.net/fileadmin/resources/research/report25.pdf

Timperley, H., Wilson, A., Barrar, H., & Fung, I. (2007). *Teacher professional learning and development: Best evidence synthesis iteration.* Wellington, New Zealand: Ministry of Education.

U.S. Congress. (2014). *Workforce Investment and Opportunity Act.* Retrieved from https://www.congress.gov/113/bills/hr803/BILLS-113hr803enr.pdf.

World Education, Inc. (2016). *System for Adult Basic Education Support FY16 Report to Massachusetts Department of Elementary and Secondary Education, Adult and Community Learning Services.* Unpublished report.

CRISTINE SMITH is an associate professor in the College of Education at the University of Massachusetts Amherst. Her research and teaching focus is on teacher professional development and literacy education for children, youth, and adults in the United States and developing countries.

8

This chapter provides brief summaries of recent research on literacy, numeracy, and language education for adults.

Research Updates: Reading, Numeracy, and Language Education

Daphne Greenberg, Lynda Ginsburg, Heide Spruck Wrigley

A definition of literacy that is commonly used in the field of adult literacy is "the ability to read, write, and speak in English, and compute and solve problems at levels of proficiency necessary to function on the job and in society, achieve one's goals, and develop one's knowledge and potential" (National Literacy Act, 1991, Section 3). This chapter focuses on three key skill areas highlighted in this definition: reading, numeracy, and language. Here, we give a brief overview of where the current emphases are in research on adults who are working to improve their skills and abilities in these areas.

Reading Research: Beyond Decoding

Expert and nonexpert readers share common goals for reading, such as making sense of the world around us, seeking entertainment, and/or following instructions. Comprehension is the vehicle that supports readers being able to reach these goals, but it is a complex activity involving many underlying components. During the past decade, most of the published research on adults who read below the ninth-grade level has focused on these underlying components of reading that contribute to comprehension; there is a paucity of research on the sociocultural aspects of reading.

It is fairly well established that adults who have low literacy skills often have difficulty with phonological awareness and decoding (e.g., Sabatini, Sawaki, Shore, & Scarborough, 2010). In the past 10 years, however, we have learned more about other reading components, such as fluency, vocabulary, and morphology. Fluency is defined as the ability to read quickly, accurately, and with correct prosody (i.e., reading with expression), leaving the reader free to focus on comprehension (Klauda & Guthrie, 2008). Fluency can be measured at the word, sentence, and/or passage levels; research has indicated that adults who struggle with reading are often deficient in all of these (MacArthur, Konold, Glutting, & Alamprese, 2010; Sabatini et al., 2010). Vocabulary consists of receptive and expressive skills. Research repeatedly shows that the receptive vocabulary knowledge of adults who have difficulty reading is more

New Directions for Adult and Continuing Education, no. 155, Fall 2017 © 2017 Wiley Periodicals, Inc.
Published online in Wiley Online Library (wileyonlinelibrary.com) • DOI: 10.1002/ace.20243

in line with their reading grade-level equivalent rather than their chronological age (e.g., Sabatini et al., 2010). Pae, Greenberg, and Williams (2012) have added nuance to these findings by demonstrating that adults with low reading skills performed better than children on "real-life" words; children do better on academic vocabulary. With regard to expressive vocabulary, Eme, Lacroix, and Almecija (2010) found that when compared to adult proficient readers, adults in basic skills classes included fewer words and word types in oral narratives. Finally, recent research on morphological awareness (the awareness of the essential "units of meaning" at the word level) has indicated that struggling adult readers have difficulty with morphologically complex words (e.g., Tighe & Binder, 2013). However, this was less pronounced when the words were presented in context.

Proficient readers do more than deploy these components to make meaning from text. For example, using background knowledge, reasoning skills, and memory are also important but have been less researched. Background knowledge helps readers make sense of text (McNamara & Magliano, 2009). However, this is not addressed systematically by researchers or by teachers of adults (Strucker, 2013). In Greenberg's research, compared to age-matched college students, adults were very deficient in background knowledge. For example, when asked how many weeks are in a year, only 10% of the adults answered the question correctly, compared to 80% of the college students (unpublished study).

Reasoning skills help readers understand text, but only one type of reasoning skill—inference—has been studied; researchers note that adults who have reading difficulties are able to make predictive inferences (Binder, Chace, & Manning, 2007). Memory is also crucial because it helps readers keep relevant information in mind and ignore information that is no longer important (e.g., Conners, 2009; Samuels, 2004). This is critical, especially as text becomes longer and more complicated. Mellard, Fall, and Woods (2010) found that adults with low literacy skills scored lower than the 10th percentile on memory tasks. More research is needed in all these areas to understand the connection between reading and background knowledge, reasoning skills, and memory, especially for adult learners who interact with increasingly complicated text as they transition into postsecondary education.

It is clear that adults attending adult basic education programs need instruction in many aspects of reading. In order to determine the best way to integrate the different components into curriculum, we need to know how these components work together to produce expert reading. Our understanding of the interrelationships among reading components relies largely on what is known about children (Miller, McCardle, & Hernandez, 2010). However, generalizing from children to adults is problematic; researchers who try to model these relationships based on what is known about children run into difficulties (see special issue of the *Journal of Learning Disabilities*, MacArthur, Greenberg, Mellard, & Sabatini, 2010). Another gap in the knowledge base on adult reading is that researchers generally have focused on conventional print literacies. Digital technologies are becoming more and more pervasive, but little is known about whether similar reading features are important for both print and digital literacies. For example, compared to print literacies, digital literacies have multiple modes involving text, image and/or sound, and are more participatory/collaborative (Knobel & Lankshear, 2014). Because of the increasing prevalence of web-based technology, adults need to be able to read web pages and social media, navigate the Internet, and use electronic devices for interacting with a wide variety of text. This makes it important for research on technology-based text interaction to inform instruction and prevent adult learners from falling further behind in their negotiation of daily literacy demands.

Regardless of the type of literacy (conventional or digital), there are many skills that adults need to master in order to become proficient readers. Reder (2009) found that adult reading gains are linked to reading engagement. Echoing this, a National Research Council (2012) report states, "Literacy is a complex skill that requires thousands of hours of practice" (p. 23). Given that consistent program attendance is difficult for many adults, it is critical to figure out ways to motivate adults to read outside the classroom. Yet, adult literacy teachers are often unaware of their students' daily reading activities (Compton-Lilly, 2009). If instructors asked students about their daily literacy engagement, this knowledge could inform instructional practices that encourages more reading (Mellard, Patterson, & Prewart, 2007). Porter, Cuban, and Comings (2005) provide suggestions on how to individualize instruction for adults to maximize their reading routines. They stress the importance of catering instruction to learners' needs and goals and showing learners how to access literacy resources. Gongora (2006) encourages the use of podcast technology for teachers to share lessons with absent students. A challenge to practitioners over the next decade is to find ways for adults to obtain reading practice, increasingly taking advantage of the affordances of technology, so that their underlying reading components can improve.

As noted earlier, there is a paucity of recent research on the sociocultural aspects of adult reading. The importance of such work is that when practitioners better understand the types of reading tasks, texts, and purposes for reading that their students have and the supports and barriers they experience as they navigate the world of print, important implications for instruction can emerge. In this way, teachers can focus on components underlying reading while also acknowledging the different sociocultural aspects of reading that should help shape each learner's experiences in the classroom. Such a marriage between a deeper understanding of the components of reading and the sociocultural aspects of reading for adults trying to improve their skills could result in more meaningful instructional experiences for learners. To achieve this, practitioners, component researchers, sociocultural researchers, and learners will need to work together to generate new knowledge and implications for practice. It is hoped that in future policymakers and grant funders will encourage this line of inquiry as we strive to help adult learners reach their reading goals.

Numeracy and Mathematics Research: Transfer Between the Workplace and the Classroom

This section reviews recent literature on adult numeracy, much of which has to do with learning for and within the workplace. The research examines the mathematical content, conceptual understanding, and mathematical practices developed in different settings, as well as the challenges of transferring learning across school, work, and everyday contexts.

There is a societal expectation that if students study mathematics in educational settings, they will easily transfer the knowledge gained to "authentic" work and life settings. Conversely, many adult educators expect that when adults return to educational settings, they bring with them "Funds of Knowledge" (Moll, Amanti, Neff, & Gonzalez, 1992) based on their lived experiences that can be used as a resource for learning. The formal and informal mathematical strategies they use in their everyday activities are assumed to be available as a basis for further mathematical learning. Therefore, by looking at numeracy practices in both educational and work settings, we should be able to identify any commonalities, potential affordances and challenges in moving between settings.

However, adults often report that they do not perform any math in their jobs, although researchers have frequently identified mathematical processes and reasoning that occur in a range of workplaces. To many, the math they do there is "invisible" (Marr & Hagston, 2007; Wedege, 2010). Ethnographic studies of auto parts manufacturing, aged-care facilities, nursing, and other settings found that workers commonly use measurement and measurement tools; graphs, charts, and tables; formulae; plans, diagrams, and scale drawings; and calculations with addition, subtraction, multiplication, percent, and ratios (Kent, Bakker, Hoyles, & Noss, 2011; Marks, Hodgen, Coben, & Bretscher, 2015; Marr & Hagston, 2007). There, mathematical practices are deeply embedded in the work environments, are setting specific, and are often learned from other workers as the way things are done. Perhaps one reason for the disconnection between employees' self-report and researchers' observations is that mathematical practices and procedures do not always reflect traditional, school-based procedures but instead rely heavily on the situational realities of particular work settings. Indeed, Keogh, Maguire, and O'Donoghue (2014) state, "Mastery of routine mathematics alone was a poor indicator of a person's ability to 'do the job'" (p. 85). Given the embedded nature of workplace numeracy, it may be unrealistic to expect workers themselves to identify and describe their mathematical practices in ways that are related to academic math. Thus, if instructors are really to prepare learners for entry to and success in work, they must be aware of and value the mathematical practices of the workplaces and explicitly weave the connections and common strategies throughout instruction.

Just like workplaces, adult education classrooms function as particular, specialized contexts with their own expectations and ways of doing things.

New Directions for Adult and Continuing Education • DOI: 10.1002/ace

One common feature of math classes is "word problems." They are promoted as providing students with preparation for numeracy problem solving outside of the classroom (see Palm, 2006, for a useful framework). But do adult learners actually use word problems as vehicles for connecting school math and real-life numeracy practices? Through recordings of learners engaged in collaborative problem solving in an adult numeracy class, Oughton (2009) found that adults did not draw on their funds of knowledge and everyday numeracy practices even though the word problems seemed to represent familiar everyday situations. Instead, they used school-like procedures and expectations to find exact answers rather than doing the estimating they would have likely used outside of school. Similarly, Sitomer (2011) found no difference in the reasonableness of solutions between older adult and traditional-aged developmental math students on open-ended word problems, though a few of the older adults explicitly referenced their out-of-school experiences. Again, this indicates that many adults do not make connections with and build on their funds of knowledge when they are in school settings. Classroom contexts may not be easily aligned with the demands and expectations of actual workplaces; instead, classroom-based learning is aligned with the demands of assessments for licensure, certification, and high school equivalency tests. Thus, math knowledge and experience do not easily transfer from the real world into the math classroom where teachers and learners could use that knowledge and experience to facilitate understanding.

Perhaps one reason that students have such difficulty benefiting from understanding developed outside of school is because their earlier school experiences have not encouraged such reasoning. Stigler, Givvin, and Thompson's (2010) analysis of more than 1,000 developmental math students' performance on an algebra readiness placement test indicated that incorrect responses reflected a history of mathematics education that primarily emphasized computational procedures with little attention to developing conceptual understanding. They suggest that, had the students reasoned at all about their answers, they would not have made the errors they did. Indeed, when asked to explain why they selected the answer they did on the multiple choice test, they frequently reverted to describing the steps of the procedure used. This suggests that students may either not have sufficient conceptual understanding of mathematical content, whether learned in earlier formal schooling or developed informally outside of school, or recognize that they *can* call upon their reasoning skills to inform their school-based activity.

Despite the challenges demonstrated by Oughton (2009) and Stigler et al. (2010), some additional research is informative for identifying effective practices for numeracy instruction in adult education classes that might lead to the development of valued workplace skills. Collaborative work as a means of effective and meaningful problem solving is embraced in the workplace but not always in adult numeracy classes. However, Martin and Towers (2012) found that in some construction trades training programs, adult students developed mathematical understanding by working collaboratively in small groups. This is accomplished through "improvisational coaction," defined as

> a process through which mathematical ideas and actions, initially stemming from an individual learner, become taken up, built upon, developed, reworked, and elaborated by others, and thus emerge as shared understandings for and across the group, rather than remaining located within any one individual. (pp. 9–10)

Oughton (2009) also saw that when adult numeracy learners work together, they admit doubt, challenge each other's responses, eliminate easy possibilities, use different forms of visualization and employ a variety of approaches. Group work is valued and promoted in the workplace and, when implemented in the classroom, can contribute to the development of mathematical understanding.

In conclusion, current research in the workplace as well as in adult numeracy classrooms suggests that development of conceptual understanding and meaningful mathematical practices benefits adults in all aspects of their lives. However, facilitating transfer across life settings continues to be challenging. Because math use is deeply embedded in workplace activities and is rarely even recognized as math, learners may not see how the math learned in the classroom is relevant. Further, learners may not understand the value of or feel empowered to bring their out-of-school math practices into classrooms. Thus, the familiar practices of their daily lives rarely inform or enrich instruction. Classroom instruction instead often focuses on mastery of "standard" procedures and abstractions that are devoid of meaning and context rather than on real-life applications and practices that resemble what is seen in the community or the workplace. The research implies that to facilitate transfer, teachers need to examine and valorize the mathematical practices and procedures used in everyday, family, community, and work settings; investigate with learners the use of alternative instructional strategies; help learners understand mathematical concepts; and help them see the connections across assessments, in everyday life, and in work settings.

Necessary But Not Sufficient: Findings in Adult English Acquisition

In the United States, as elsewhere, learning and teaching another language are closely tied to immigrant integration and efforts to help foreign-born families adjust to a new environment and a new society (National Academy of Sciences, 2015; Wrigley, 2012). As a result of this emphasis, available research tends to focus less on the linguistic aspects of language development (syntax, morphology, phonology, vocabulary) and more on issues related to teaching/learning and program implementation.

The study of adult language acquisition is complex and few university-based researchers have the experience or resources to disentangle the many factors that affect the development of language proficiency. Variables that influence learning include the degree of literacy in the native language, as well as the interaction between conversational competence and print literacy. Immigration and employment status, length of time in the country and the degree of exposure to English also play an important role in determining how quickly individuals learn English or how fluent they become; the most important variable, perhaps, is access to a high-quality, learner-centered program tailored an individual's needs. This is difficult to find in a field that is notoriously underfunded and where only about 3% of immigrants who could benefit from English courses are served in federally funded programs (Park, McHugh, & Katsiaficas, 2016).

The sheer diversity of languages spoken by immigrants learning English poses a significant challenge to researchers; surveys, interviews, and assessments used for research purposes need to be translated. For studies focused on adults who have low or no literacy skills in their first language, qualified interpreters who are aware of the linguistic and cultural backgrounds of learners may need to be involved (Wrigley, 2013).

In part as a result of these challenges, instead of traditional studies carried out by university researchers using controlled experimental and survey designs, the research in the adult English as a another language field is dominated by policy studies or mixed-methods designs that often lack relevance to practice (Condelli & Wrigley, 2008). This section offers an overview of this research that speaks to the role of English in immigrant integration, making an important distinction between low-skilled and high-skilled foreign-born adults.

The Importance of English Proficiency. The U.S. government has identified three pillars of immigrant integration: linguistic, economic, and civic integration. English proficiency is shown to be an important factor in all three dimensions. The relationship is most researched in the area of economic integration and the data the strongest, although other studies highlight the barriers posed by low English proficiency in the areas of parent engagement in schools.

Several studies provide clear evidence that higher wages are correlated with higher levels of English proficiency (Bergson-Shilcock & Witte, 2015; McHugh & Morawski, 2017). This correlation holds true for both low-skilled adults, those with less than a high school education, and foreign-born professionals, those with college degrees. The relationship between English proficiency and civic engagement is somewhat more tenuous with indications that voting behavior is influenced by both competence in English and years of schooling (immigrants with higher levels of education and English proficiency vote at a higher rate). We can expect that the same is true for other forms of civic participation (National Academy of Sciences, 2015).

Current research underscores the importance of English proficiency; yet there have been few studies that provide insights into what evidence-based practices help English learners make progress and achieve important integration goals, such as obtaining a job that pays a living wage, fully participating in civic life, and/or supporting the educational success of their children.

Effective Practices. Research on effective approaches to delivering English language education to adult immigrants is extremely limited; so much so that the National Research Council (NRC) included studies conducted with English language learners in high schools along with studies of children with limited proficiency in English in their review of promising practices in adult English acquisition (National Research Council, 2012). This report does highlight the importance of building content knowledge for learners with limited or interrupted schooling, taking advantage of first language literacy and past educational and professional experience, and taking into account the sociocultural and affective dimensions of language learning. The NRC also highlighted approaches to language teaching and learning based on evidence from the field rather than from empirical research. These included methods that focus both on language form (i.e., the structure of English) and meaning (understanding and self-expression), task-based instruction, and explicit teaching of strategies and skills. The NRC cautions that, given the wide range of learners and the myriad purposes for learning English, one size is not likely to fit all and calls for research with subgroups, such as low literate adults and more highly skilled immigrants.

Adult Language Learners with Low Levels of Education. For beginning-level English learners, a national study, What Works in Adult ESL Literacy (Condelli & Wrigley, 2008), points to several instructional strategies found to promote progress in English acquisition. These strategies include connecting classroom teaching to learners' lives, using the native language to explain unclear points and in discussions, and offering a variety of practices and modalities to engage learners (Wrigley, 2003).

Studies exploring the relationship between English proficiency and workforce success (Jacoby, 2015; Spence, 2010; Wrigley, Richer, Martinson, Kubo, & Strawn, 2003) make it clear that increasing the English language skills of lower educated immigrants is necessary but not sufficient to help adults get jobs with living wages and achieve economic integration. For many, the path into the middle class will require continued participation in programs that combine English language acquisition and job skills training (Unruh & Bergson-Shilcock, 2015; Wrigley, 2015). Unfortunately, most training programs are not geared toward students who do not yet speak English well. This lack of access to programs that combine job training and English acquisition delays not only linguistic and economic integration but social mobility as well (Spence, 2010.)

Recent legislation, the Workforce Investment and Opportunity Act (WIOA), is likely to slow not only economic integration for low-skilled immigrants but linguistic and civic integration for those without employment goals. The strong emphasis of WIOA on performance outcomes related to employment and training and transition to postsecondary education is likely to

New Directions for Adult and Continuing Education • DOI: 10.1002/ace

make adult education programs "risk averse" (McHugh, 2017), choosing to give priority to higher skilled adults more likely to progress on these metrics. Narrow accountability measures will make programs less eager to serve immigrants who are beginning-level learners not ready for job skills training, parents of small children not in the labor market, and those wanting to learn English to gain citizenship, learn to navigate social and government systems, and engage more fully in their communities (McHugh & Morawski, 2016) College-Educated Immigrants.

Although the majority of English learners in the United States have low levels of education (significantly lower than native-born adults), about one third of immigrants have a bachelor's degree or higher (similar to native-born adults). In recent years, several studies have focused on the lack of language education opportunities for college-educated immigrants whose English is still imperfect (Bergson-Shilcock & Witte, 2015; McHugh & Morawski, 2017). The economic success of higher skilled individuals depends on a number of factors, including time in the country, levels of acculturation, and access to recredentialing services. The most significant determinant of success is the same as for their lower educated counterparts: English proficiency (Bergson-Shilcock &Witte, 2015; McHugh & Morawski, 2017; Zong & Batalova, 2016). Without increased English skills, those with limited English cannot fully use the knowledge and skill gained in training in their home countries in U.S. work or community contexts. As a result, college-educated immigrants with limited English tend to be seriously underemployed, working in low-skilled jobs, and making significantly less money than their English-speaking peers with similar educational attainment. These studies also note that there are few publicly funded classes available that teach business English or English for professional purposes for students who are not yet fully literate or proficient in English.

Given the continued influx of immigrants to the United States, we would hope to see a great deal more research examining the various dimensions of adult English acquisition. Yet, given the anti-immigrant and antirefugee discourse of the current administration, there is little hope that significant funding will be available for these types of studies. As things stand, we still have a limited understanding of what it takes to support adult English language learners from different groups to develop the kind of proficiency that would allow them to meet their personal and professional goals and achieve linguistic, economic, and civic integration. Given the many factors influencing second language acquisition (cognitive, linguistic, affective), it is perhaps not surprising that there is little academic research. This paucity is exacerbated by practically no funding for such research. In the meantime, implementation studies providing insights into both barriers and promising practices that foster success will have to suffice. In the end, widespread advocacy efforts will be needed to expand language services in both quantity and quality to help immigrants learning English not only to survive, but to thrive (Wrigley, 2008).

Conclusion

Although reading, numeracy, and English language proficiency can be thought of as very disparate subjects, they share common themes in the field of adult literacy research. The chapter brings out the complexities in unpacking larger literacy constructs into their subparts. For example, literacy is not just reading, and reading is just not phonics. In addition, the authors highlight the importance of recognizing the role of context, social cultural issues, and authentic use of skills and knowledge both in and out of the classroom setting. Finally, they all stress the lack of research in their respective areas, and the impact that this dearth has on the quality of instruction.

References

Bergson-Shilcock, A., & Witte, J. (2015). *Steps to success: Integrating immigrant professionals in the US*. New York, NY: World Education Services and IMPRINT.

Binder, K., Chace, K., & Manning, M. (2007). Sentential and discourse context effects: adults who are learning to read compared with skilled readers. *Journal of Research in Reading, 30*, 360–378.

Compton-Lilly, C. (2009). Disparate reading identities of adult students in one GED program. *Adult Basic Education and Literacy Journal, 3*(1), 34–43.

Condelli, L., & Wrigley, H. S. (2008). What Works Study: Instruction, literacy and language learning for adult ESL literacy students. In S. Reder & J. Bynner (Eds.), *Tracking adult literacy and numeracy skills: Findings from longitudinal research* (pp. 133–159). London & New York: Routledge.

Conners, F. A. (2009). Attentional control and the simple view of reading. *Reading and Writing, 22*, 591–613. https://doi.org/10.1007/s11145-008-9126-x

Eme, E., Lacroix, A., & Almecija, Y. (2010). Oral narrative skills in French adults who are functionally illiterate: Linguistic features and discourse organization. *Journal of Speech, Language, and Hearing Research, 53*,1349–1371. https://doi.org/10.1044/1092-4388(2010/08-0092

Gongora, K.M. (2006, Fall). Audio to go: A podcasting primer. *LitScape*, p. 3.

Jacoby, T. (2015). *What works: English learning in America*. New York, NY: Manhattan Institute.

Kent, P., Bakker, A., Hoyles, C., & Noss, R. (2011). Measurement in the workplace: The case of process improvement in the manufacturing industry. *ZDM—The International Journal on Mathematics Education, 43*(5), 747–758.

Keogh, J. J., Maguire, T., & O'Donoghue, J. (2014). A workplace contextualization of mathematics: Measuring workplace context complexity. *Adults Learning Mathematics: An International Journal, 9*(1), 85–99.

Klauda, S., & Guthrie, J. (2008). Relationships of three components of reading fluency to reading comprehension. *Journal of Educational Psychology, 100*, 310–321.

Knobel, M., & Lankshear, C. (2014). Studying new literacies. *Journal of Adolescent & Adult Literacy, 58*(2), 97–101. https://doi.org/10.1002/jaal.314

MacArthur, C., Greenberg, D., Mellard, D. F., & Sabatini, J. P. (Eds.). (2010). Models of reading component skills in low-literate adults [Special issue]. *Journal of Learning Disabilities, 43*(2).

MacArthur, C., Konold, T., Glutting, J., & Alamprese, J. (2010). Reading component skills of learners in adult basic education. *Journal of Learning Disabilities, 43*, 108–121.

New Directions for Adult and Continuing Education • DOI: 10.1002/ace

Marks, R., Hodgen, J., Coben, D., & Bretscher, N. (2015). Nursing students' experiences of learning numeracy for professional practice. *Adults Learning Mathematics: An International Journal*, *11*(1), 43–58.

Marr, B., & Hagston, J. (2007). *Thinking beyond numbers: Numeracy for the future workplace. Adult literacy national project report.* Adelaide, Australia: National Centre for Vocational Education Research.

Martin, L., & Towers, J. (2012). "Some guys wouldn't use three-eights on anything…": Improvisational coaction in an apprenticeship training classroom. *Adults Learning Mathematics: An International Journal*, *7*(1), 8–19.

McHugh, M. (2017). *Ensuring immigrants' access to WIOA: Data and advocacy for adult educators.* Syracuse, NY: Coalition on Adult Basic Education.

McHugh, M., & Morawski, M. (2016). *Immigrants and WIOA services: Comparison of sociodemographic characteristics of native- and foreign-born adults in the United States.* Washington, DC: Migration Policy Institute.

McHugh, M., & Morawski, M. (2017). *Unlocking skills: Successful initiatives for integrating foreign-trained immigrant professionals.* Washington, DC: Migration Policy Institute.

McNamara, D. S., & Magliano, J. P. (2009). Towards a comprehensive model of comprehension. In B. Ross (Ed.), *The psychology of learning and motivation* (pp. 297–384). New York, NY: Elsevier Science.

Mellard, D., Fall, E., & Woods, K. (2010). A path analysis of reading comprehension of adults with low literacy. *Journal of Learning Disabilities*, *43*, 154–195. https://doi.org/10.1177/0022219409359345

Mellard, D. F., Patterson, M. B., & Prewett, S., (2007). Reading practices among adult education participants. *Reading Research Quarterly*, *42*, 188–213.

Miller, B., McCardle, P. & Hernandez, R. (2010). Advances and remaining challenges in adult literacy research. *Journal of Learning Disabilities*, *43*, 101–107.

Moll, L. C., Amanti, C., Neff, D., & Gonzalez, N. (1992). Funds of knowledge for teaching: Using a qualitative approach to connect homes and classrooms. *Theory into Practice*, *31*(2), 132–141.

National Academy of Sciences. (2015). *The integration of immigrants into American society.* Washington, DC: National Academies Press.

National Literacy Act of 1991, Public Law 102–73, Section 3. Retrieved from https://www.gpo.gov/fdsys/pkg/STATUTE-105/pdf/STATUTE-105-Pg333.pdf

National Research Council. (2012). Improving adult literacy instruction: Options for practice and research. Committee on Learning Sciences: Foundations and Applications to Adolescent and Adult Literacy, A.M. Lesgold & M. Welch-Ross (Eds.) *Division of Behavioral and Social Sciences and Education.* Washington, DC: The National Academies Press.

Oughton, H. (2009). A willing suspension of disbelief? "Contexts" and recontextualisation in adult numeracy classrooms. *Adults Learning Mathematics: An International Journal*, *4*(1), 16–31.

Pae, H., Greenberg, D., & Williams, R. (2012). An analysis of differential response patterns on the Peabody Picture Vocabulary Test-III in adult struggling readers and third-grade children. *Reading and Writing: An Interdisciplinary Journal*, *25*, 1239–1258. https://doi.org/10.1007/s11145-011-9315-x

Palm, T. (2006). Word problems as simulations of real-world situations: A proposed framework. *For the Learning of Mathematics*, *26*(1), 42–47.

Park, M., McHugh, M., & Katsiaficas, C. (2016). *Serving immigrant families through two-generation programs: Identifying family needs and responsive program approaches.* Washington, DC: Migration Policy Institute.

Porter, K. E., Cuban, S., & Comings, J. P. (2005, January). *"One day I will make it." A study of adult student persistence in library literacy programs.* New York. NY: MDRC.

Reder, S. (2009). Scaling up and moving in: Connecting social practices views to policies and programs in adult education. *Literacy and Numeracy Studies*, *16*(2) & *17*(1), 35–50.

Sabatini, J., Sawaki, Y., Shore, J., & Scarborough, H. (2010). Relationships among reading skills of adults with low literacy. *Journal of Learning Disabilities, 43*, 122–138. https://doi.org/10.1177/0022219409359343

Samuels, S. (2004). Toward a theory of automatic information processing in reading, revisited. In R. Ruddell, & N. Unrau (Eds.), *Theoretical models and processes of reading* (pp. 1127–1148). Newark, DE: International Reading Association.

Sitomer, A. (2011). Exploring the influence of life and school on mathematical problem solving. In *Proceedings of the 17th International Conference of Adults Learning Mathematics: A Research Forum* (pp. 160–168). Oslo, Norway: Vox/ALM.

Spence, R. (2010). *Sound investments: Building immigrants' skills to fuel economic growth.* New York: Economic Mobility Corporation.

Stigler, J. W., Givvin, K. B., & Thompson, B. J. (2010). What community college developmental mathematics students understand about mathematics. *MathAMATYC Educator, 1*(3), 4–16.

Strucker, J. (2013). The knowledge gap and adult learners. *Perspectives on Language and Literacy, 39*, 25–28.

Tighe, E. L., & Binder, K. (2013). An investigation of morphological awareness and processing in adults with low literacy. *Applied Psycholinguistics*, 1–29. https://doi.org/10.1017/S0142716413000222.

Unruh, R. B.-S. (2015). *Missing in action: Job-driven educational pathways for unauthorized youth and adults.* New York, NY: National Skills Coalition.

Wedege, T. (2010). People's mathematics in working life: Why is it invisible? *Adults Learning Mathematics: An International Journal, 5*(1), 89–97.

Wrigley, H. (2003, September). What works for adult ESL students: A conversation with Focus on Basics. *Focus on Basics, 6*(C), 14–17.

Wrigley, H. (2008). From survival to thriving. In I. Van de Craats & J. Kurvers (Eds.), *Low educated adult second language literacy acquisition. Proceedings of the 4th Symposium Antwerp 2008* (pp. 71–84). Utrecht: Netherlands Graduate School of Linguistics.

Wrigley, H. S. (2012). Dimensions of immigrant integration and civic engagement: Issues and exemplary programs. In L. Munoz & H. S. Wrigley (Eds.), *Adult civic engagement in adult learning* (pp. 25–32). San Francisco: Jossey-Bass.

Wrigley, H. S. (2013). New to literacy: Challenges facing immigrant and refugee adults with little prior schooling. *Perspectives on Language and Literacy, 39*(2), 31–34.

Wrigley, H. (2015). *Preparing English learners for work and career pathways.* Washington, DC: Literacy Information and Communication System (LINCS).

Wrigley, H., Richer, E., Martinson, K., Kubo, H., & Strawn, J. (2003). *The language of opportunity: Expanding employment prospects for adults with limited English skills.* Washington, DC: Center for Law and Social Policy.

Zong, J., & Batalova, J. (2016). *College educated immigrants in the United States.* Washington, DC: Migration Policy Institute.

DAPHNE GREENBERG, Ph.D., is a Distinguished University Professor in Educational Psychology and director of the Adult Literacy Research Center at Georgia State University, Atlanta, Georgia.

LYNDA GINSBURG, Ph.D., is a senior research associate for Mathematics Education, Center for Math, Science and Computer Education, Rutgers University, Piscataway, New Jersey.

HEIDE SPRUCK WRIGLEY, Ph.D., is senior researcher with Literacywork International based in Mesilla, NM. She is a nonresident fellow with the Migration Policy Institute.

9

This chapter identifies directions for future ABE research and suggests how researchers and practitioners can enrich the field's knowledge base.

Conclusion

Esther Prins

This volume covers myriad issues, practices, and policies that have shaped the contours of adult basic education (ABE) in the United States and that will invariably shape its future. This chapter delineates salient gaps in the ABE research base and suggests how researchers and practitioners can mutually enrich the field's knowledge base. The thin research base is an oft-noted problem. Particularly lacking is research that can inform practice and thus help policymakers, practitioners, and administrators make wise, well-informed decisions about how to organize programs and implement instruction so that adult learners can flourish.

Research Gaps

The preceding chapters simultaneously expand our knowledge about their respective topics, raise new questions, and expose gaps in the empirical research base. I begin by outlining several areas for future research. These ideas are intended to be suggestive, not exhaustive, and are also shaped by my own scholarly expertise and interests.

Rural–Urban Disparities. The distinctive experiences and challenges of ABE in rural areas are largely neglected in education and adult education research. The geographic setting shapes access to resources such as higher and adult education, living-wage jobs, and the internet; community residents' educational trajectories; adult learners' prospects for entering postsecondary education or securing employment; adult learners' literacy and numeracy practices; and much more. For instance, McLendon (Chapter 4) shows that adult educators' resistance to the GED Testing Service's computerized test stemmed largely from concerns about rural programs' and adult learners' limited computer access.

In absolute terms, most adults who struggle with literacy, numeracy, or English language live in urban areas; however, average education levels are far lower in rural communities. Geographic disparities in access to education (especially postsecondary) help explain why only one in five rural,

New Directions for Adult and Continuing Education, no. 155, Fall 2017 © 2017 Wiley Periodicals, Inc.
Published online in Wiley Online Library (wileyonlinelibrary.com) • DOI: 10.1002/ace.20244

working-age adults has a college degree, compared to one in three urban residents (U.S. Department of Agriculture Economic Research Service, 2015). Compared to urban areas, rural communities have higher poverty and disability rates, lower rates of job growth, and high rates of self-employed entrepreneurs (Thiede, Greiman, Weiler, Beda, & Conroy, 2017), all of which have implications for ABE.

Place structures people's life opportunities; we need more research showing how it matters specifically in ABE. This research can, in turn, inform efforts to help rural adults take advantage of adult education to pursue their goals and enrich their lives and communities. My prior research elucidates some of the ways that rurality shapes adult education and the experiences and characteristics of adult learners (e.g., Prins & Kassab, 2015; Prins, Kassab, Drayton, & Gungor, 2012; Prins & Toso, 2012). Given dwindling state and federal funding for ABE, we need more research documenting the experiences and challenges of rural adults who have the least access to ABE programs, higher education, and employment.

Immigrants and Refugees. A second salient research topic is immigrants and refugees in ABE (Larrotta, Chapter 6; Greenberg, Ginsburg, & Wrigley, Chapter 8). The recent executive orders on immigrants and refugees have profound implications for programs and learners, including funding, student recruitment and retention, curricular content, and strategies for helping participants who fear for their future. As of August 2017, federal judges had blocked most of President Trump's travel ban, but its effects are already being felt. Illegal border crossings from Mexico into the United States declined by 36% from February 2016 to February 2017 (Kulish & Santos, 2018). In February 2017, World Relief, a refugee resettlement agency, closed five offices and laid off 140 staff due to the reduced number of refugees permitted to enter the country. A Pennsylvania Association for Adult Education email reported that immigrant students and staff were "becoming extremely upset over the travel ban and changes to Immigration and Customs Enforcement procedures" and that programs have responded by offering counseling and referring participants to community organizations (personal communication, March 6, 2017). It is safe to assume that similar scenarios are playing out nationally.

Researchers need to document how ABE and English as a Second Language programs and participants are responding to the executive orders, deportation actions, anti-immigrant sentiments, and the challenges and anxiety these engender. Duffy (2007) described how Hmong refugees in rural Wisconsin adopted new literacy practices such as writing letters to the editor to educate the public about their culture, history, and values and to contest negative public perceptions of the Hmong. This example points to the importance of researching how immigrants and refugees today are deploying their literacy abilities to advocate and educate and how ABE programs can foster their ability to use language and literacy to counter prejudice and discrimination. Given the current climate, research documenting the role of adult education in immigrants' and refugees' successful integration is especially vital.

New Directions for Adult and Continuing Education • DOI: 10.1002/ace

College and Career Readiness Standards for Adult Education. Researchers should problematize the College and Career Readiness Standards (CCRS) for Adult Education (Pimentel, 2013) and examine the intended and unintended consequences of their adoption, including how they are shaping instruction. Because the Common Core State Standards (CCSS)—the basis for the CCRS—have been widely critiqued (e.g., Smith, Appleman, & Wilhelm, 2014), it is surprising that few adult education researchers have problematized the CCRS. For example, the CCRS may contribute to the "narrowing" that Belzer (Chapter 1) describes, with employment and higher education eclipsing other purposes for literacy and numeracy learning.

I focus on one aspect of the CCRS to illustrate my point: the emphasis on reading nonfiction, informational text. "Knowledge: building knowledge through content-rich nonfiction" (Pimentel, 2013, p. 10) is one of three "key shifts" in the Common Core and the CCRS. CCRS panelists included reading standards related to informational text "principally because expository text makes up the vast majority of the required reading most students will face in college and the workplace" (p. 105). Although being able to read and understand informational text is important, this shift may also have unintended instructional consequences.

Both the CCSS and the adult education standards claim that they "do not specify how instructors should teach" (Pimentel, 2013, p. 8). Yet, Mooney (2015) shows that the CCSS *do* shape teaching. For instance, an elementary school teacher used a nonfiction text about Abraham Lincoln but focused only on developing the intended CCSS skill—using text evidence—rather than also discussing substantive issues therein. The shift toward informational text refers to "building knowledge," yet the only knowledge the teachers mentioned was knowledge of CCSS-required skills such as providing text evidence (p. 127).

Understanding informational text also requires specific vocabulary and background knowledge. Elementary teachers in Ness's (2011) study reported that beginning readers and English learners struggled with the "demanding vocabulary," "language demands," and background knowledge required to comprehend informational text (p. 42). Although we must be cautious about applying K–12 research to ABE, these studies underscore the importance of examining how the CCRS are shaping ABE instruction. For instance, what are the implications of the CCRS's shift toward informational text? Have adult educators narrowed their focus to teach the CCRS skills? What kinds of challenges do informational texts present for ABE students? What kinds of background knowledge are needed to understand informational texts, and what kinds of strategies help compensate for gaps and expand learners' background knowledge? (Greenberg et al., this volume, report that adult learners have less background knowledge than their same-age peers.) In sum, the CCRS warrant much closer examination of implementation and consequences in ABE.

Digital Literacies. The emphasis on technology and digital literacy in several chapters (Rosen & Vanek; Greenberg et al.) points to the need for more research in this area. This transcends topics such as technology use in ABE instruction and teaching participants how to use computers and solve technologically complex problems, a skill measured by PIAAC (Stein, Chapter 3). New Literacy Studies (NLS) and multiliteracies scholarship offers relevant theoretical frameworks for researching digital literacies in ABE, but to date there has been little cross-over between these fields. In brief, NLS and multiliteracies research emphasizes the increasingly multimodal (especially visual) nature of communication (Kress, 2003) and documents how learners use digital tools to produce multimodal texts and craft new identities (Hull & Katz, 2006; Pahl, 2011).

This analytical and instructional focus diverges from the prevailing emphasis on traditional, text-based reading in ABE. We need to prepare adult learners not only to understand and consume texts but also to create them because, as Kress (2003) argues, "the power to make and disseminate meanings" is "a redistribution of semiotic power" (p. 17). This is especially important "for people whose voices often go unheard" (Pahl, 2011, p. 24). We need more research showing how digital tools are being used not only to develop technology skills such as those included in the CCRS standards (e.g., using technology to produce and publish writing; Pimentel, 2013), but also foster new kinds of learning, storytelling, and individual and community action.

An increasingly popular digital text is digital storytelling (DST), which combines communicative modes such as video clips, photos, written text, oral narration, and music. My research with a family literacy program in Ireland illustrates how a DST class enabled parents to access technological "knowledge and skills," affirmed their "diverse knowledge, languages, life experiences, and identities," and equipped them "to design and disseminate their digital stories" (Prins, 2017, p. 308). DST is well suited to ABE because English language learners, beginning writers, and adults who lack confidence as writers can combine written text with other communicative modes, especially visual ones, thus offering alternate, nonverbal routes for self-expression (Prins, 2017). In addition, the practical knowledge and skills gained through DST or other digital texts are intertwined with learners' identities (Hull & Katz, 2006; Prins, 2017). The proliferation of digital technologies calls for more research on how they are being incorporated into ABE and how adult learners use these tools to tell their stories and exercise more power over their lives.

Writing. The importance of learning to produce digital texts is related to another research gap: writing. Because of the predominant emphasis on reading in ABE, there is far less research on writing. This may be no accident. According to Deborah Brandt (2015), writing has historically been viewed as more powerful and subversive than reading and therefore more strictly regulated, with fewer "civic protections" (p. 3). For instance, the right to write and publish was excised from the final draft of the Bill of Rights, and early mass literacy campaigns excluded writing.

We have entered an era of mass writing in which more people than ever write in their daily lives and as part of their paid work (Brandt, 2015). The internet and digital technologies have catapulted writing to the forefront via texting, blogs, Facebook, participation in online communities, and more. Thus, we are now a "nation of writers....For perhaps the first time in the history of mass literacy, writing seems to be eclipsing reading as the literate experience of consequence" (Brandt, 2015, p. 3). This trend accentuates the importance of being able to write for varied purposes, especially for ABE participants who wish to secure employment and pursue postsecondary education, to tell their stories, and to advocate for themselves, their families, and their communities.

Writing features prominently in the CCRS, and for good reason:

> The rise of mass writing has accompanied the emergence of the so-called knowledge or information economy . . . .In this economy texts serve as a chief means of production and a chief output of production, and writing becomes a dominant form of manufacturing. (Brandt, 2015, p. 3)

Because writing and economic productivity are inextricably linked, writing abilities are crucial for ABE students to obtain jobs, especially better paying ones—although the labor market determines the availability of such jobs. Researchers should investigate how this new era of mass writing is reconfiguring ABE participants' prospects for different kinds of employment, how they use writing at work, and how they see themselves as writers, vis-à-vis their roles as workers.

Brandt's observations that "Writing is a site of intellectual, moral, and civic development" (p. 162) and that contemporary mass literacy development depends on learning to write and produce texts with peers raises other questions for researchers to pursue. How are ABE programs teaching writing, and what kinds of writing are being taught? How do these writing genres and activities relate to adult experiences with writing in work, education, and other domains such as parenting, citizenship, health, or self-expression, and how do they shape whether and how ABE participants see themselves as belonging to a nation of writers? How are peer teaching and feedback incorporated into writing instruction? ABE would benefit from more studies on instruction, uses, and implications of writing for multiple purposes. Because the ability to author texts is a vital way to exercise power, it would be short-sighted only to focus on the instrumental uses of writing in the workplace and educational settings.

Meeting Needs of Learners Across the Academic Spectrum. This volume documents the challenge of simultaneously serving learners with the greatest academic needs *and* meeting accountability standards emphasizing transitions to postsecondary education and employment. Jacobson (Chapter 2) notes that current success metrics may encourage programs to "cream" and limit access to students least likely to have rapid positive outcomes. This concern is affirmed in my current research on career pathways programs; practitioners have described growing pressure to recruit participants who are more likely to boost outcomes in areas such as obtaining or retaining employment, entering postsecondary education, and making gains on standardized tests. Similarly, a 2008 focus group with Pennsylvania family literacy staff revealed that accountability standards, coupled with changes in funding and related policies, made some staff hesitant to enroll families that could "bring down your averages" (Prins & Gungor, 2011, p. 22). These concerns are related to Mooney's (2015) finding that the CCSS and standardized testing encouraged teachers to focus on the "bubble kids"—students who are on the verge of passing to the next proficiency level—rather than students further from the threshold (p. 138).

Concerns about accountability pressures and "creaming" suggest myriad research topics, including the extent to which this is occurring; other unintended consequences of increased accountability and a narrow focus on employment; how programs are attempting to meet accountability standards while also meeting the needs of students for whom attending college or obtaining living-wage employment is a far-off goal (or not a goal at all); and whether career pathways programs that prepare students for employment and postsecondary education are accessible to adults who lack a high school diploma or have lower test scores (Prins et al., 2017).

Programs are not only trying to meet the needs of beginning-level ABE students but are also increasingly focused on helping more advanced students enter postsecondary education (Jacobson, this volume). Adults without a college degree bear the brunt of economic downturns and experience higher rates of poverty and unemployment, which in turn contribute to problems with mental and physical health, marital instability, food insecurity, and so on. Although enrolling in college is crucial, researchers should also recognize that the primary causes of U.S. poverty are the labor market structure (lack of living-wage jobs) and an inadequate social safety net (Rank, 2004), not the skills gap (Cappelli, 2015; Jacobson, 2016).

Recent PIAAC analyses highlight the importance of attending college, above and beyond developing one's literacy and numeracy abilities. Baker and colleagues' (2015) research shows that among adults who work full-time, higher PIAAC scores were associated with higher earnings only for those with "some college" or higher, not among adults with a high school degree. Two additional (unpublished) models including (a) adults without a high school degree and (b) adults who were employed full- or part-time yielded similar findings, except that higher PIAAC scores were related to lower earnings for adults with less than "some college" education (David Baker, personal communication, February 6, 2016; Baker noted that the number of adults without a high school degree is small, so outliers can influence the results). In other words, unless adults have at least some college education, increasing literacy and numeracy scores alone may not lead to higher earnings. These findings accentuate the need to prepare ABE participants for successful completion of college classes and to investigate how ABE participation affects employment, earnings, and economic well-being, with or without postsecondary study.

ABE and the New Federal Budget. The President's proposed 2018 federal budget raises many questions about what will happen to ABE programs and participants under an administration whose stated goal is "deconstruction of the administrative state" (Fisher, 2017). The proposal reduces WIOA Title II adult education state grants by $96 million (16%), coupled with steep cuts in-or elimination of-federal funding for workforce, human services, and education programs that benefit adult learners and people in poverty (National Skills Coalition, 2017). These include reductions in welfare and food stamps, grants for dislocated workers, apprenticeships, ex-offenders, and career technical education, and elimination of the Community Services Block Grant, among others. The budget consistently eliminates programs that have weak evidence of effectiveness and meeting objectives, which points to the need for rigorous research in ABE to demonstrate effectiveness and for measures that adequately capture adult learners' gains. However, it would be naive to assume that strong evidence of effectiveness would necessarily save an educational (or any other) program that policymakers are determined to cut based on ideology.

In brief, researchers need to document how ABE programs and personnel respond to the new budget and its consequences for adult learners, especially those who are most vulnerable. Questions about who loses and who gains and how decisions are made about allocating scarce resources with what consequences are crucial.

Working Together to Understand and Enhance ABE

In this concluding section I offer some reflections based on my recent experience working on a researcher–practitioner partnership. It has been invaluable for learning how adult education providers are implementing career pathways, how policies shape their work, and how participants are experiencing these programs. In addition, practitioners in our case studies and focus groups have identified pressing research topics including what happens to students after they complete career pathways programs. The interaction and cross-fertilization we have experienced as researcher and practitioner partners has contributed in meaningful ways to highlighting important gaps in the knowledge base for the field.

With or without grants to sustain these partnerships, researchers and practitioners must find ways to work together, to identify meaningful problems of practice, to document and learn from field-based inquiries, and to offer insights and ongoing professional development based on the resulting findings. There are many nontraditional research methods that researchers could employ to shape ABE practice, involve practitioners and participants in research, and document their knowledge, including practitioner research (Lytle, Belzer, & Reumann, 1993), action research (Greenwood & Levin, 1998), and practitioner profiles (Peters, Grégoire, & Hittleman, 2004), among others. Such projects are often situated in university–community partnerships, which bring their own set of challenges as partners navigate differing roles, expectations, goals, and forms of knowledge.

I conclude with Flyvbjerg's (2006) argument that research resulting in practical, "concrete, context-dependent knowledge" (p. 223) is often more valuable than research focused on generalizable, predictive theories. The former—*phronesis*, or practical wisdom—is precisely what the ABE field needs in these times.

References

Baker, D., Ford, K., Sun, L. S., Fu, Y. C., Fernandez, F., & Umbricht, M. (2015). *The educational and cognitive transformation of social opportunity and inequality: Credentials, cognition, and C-status.* Paper presented at the What We Need Skills For: the PIAAC Research Conference 2015, Arlington, VA. Retrieved from https://static1.squarespace.com/static/51bb74b8e4b0139570ddf020/t/5679a519df40f3a5265510fc/1450812697511/01_Dec 10_Baker_Ford_Draft_PPT_2015_11_23.pdf

Brandt, D. (2015). *The rise of writing.* Cambridge, UK: Cambridge University Press.

Cappelli, P. H. (2015). Skill gaps, skill shortages, and skill mismatches evidence and arguments for the united states. *ILR Review, 68*(2), 251–290.

Duffy, J. (2007). *Writing from these roots: Literacy in a Hmong-American community.* Honolulu, HI: University of Hawaii Press.

Fisher, M. (2017, February 24). Stephen K. Bannon's CPAC comments, annotated and explained. *New York Times.* Retrieved from https://www.nytimes.com/2017/02/24/us/politics/stephen-bannon-cpac-speech.html?_r = 0

Flyvbjerg, B. (2006). Five misunderstandings about case-study research. *Qualitative Inquiry, 12*(2), 219–245.

Greenwood, D., & Levin, M. (1998). *An introduction to action research: Social research for social change.* Thousand Oaks, CA: Sage.

Hull, G. A., & Katz, M.-L. (2006). Crafting an agentive self: Case studies of digital storytelling. *Research in the Teaching of English, 41*(1), 43–81. https://doi.org/10.2307/40171717

Jacobson, E. (2016). Workforce development rhetoric and the realities of 21st century capitalism. *Literacy and Numeracy Studies, 24*(1), 3–22.

Kress, G. (2003). *Literacy in the new media age.* New York, NY: Psychology Press.

Kulish, N., & Santos, F. (2018, March 8). Illegal border crossings appear to drop under Trump. *New York Times.* Retrieved from https://www.nytimes.com/2017/03/08/us/trump-immigration-border.html?_r = 0

Lytle, S., Belzer, A., & Reumann, R. (1993). *Initiating inquiry: Adult literacy teachers, tutors, and administrators research their practice (No. TR93-11).* Philadelphia, PA: National Center on Adult Literacy.

Mooney, A. (2015). *(Un)intended outcomes of the Common Core English Language Arts Standards: A narrative inquiry into the learning experiences of English learners' teachers.* Unpublished doctoral dissertation, Pennsylvania State University, University Park, PA.

National Skills Coalition. (2017). Trump FY 2018 budget slashes funding for key workforce, education, and human services programs. Retrieved from http://www.national skillscoalition.org/news/blog/trump-fy-2018-budget-slashes-funding-for-key-workforce-education-human-services-programs

Ness, M. (2011). Teachers' use of and attitudes toward informational text in K–5 classrooms. *Reading Psychology, 32*(1), 28–53.

Pahl, K. (2011). My family, my story: Representing identities in time and space through digital storytelling. *Yearbook of the National Society for the Study of Education, 110*(1), 17–39.

Peters, S. J., Grégoire, H., & Hittleman, M. (2004). Practicing a pedagogy of hope: Practitioner profiles as tools for grounding and guiding collective reflection in adult, community, and youth development education. In M. Reynolds & R. Vince (Eds.), *Organizing reflection* (pp. 194–219). Aldershot, UK: Ashgate.

Pimentel, S. (2013). *College and career readiness standards for adult education.* Washington, DC: U.S. Department of Education, Office of Vocational and Adult Education.

Prins, E. (2017). Digital storytelling in adult education and family literacy: A case study from rural Ireland. *Learning, Media and Technology, 42*(3), 308–323.

Prins, E., Clymer, C., Elder, S. F., Needle, M., Raymond, B., & Toso, B. W. (2017). *Adult education and career pathways in Chicago, Houston, and Miami.* Paper presented at the Coalition of Adult Basic Education Conference, Orlando, FL. Retrieved from https://sites.psu.edu/adultpathways/files/2015/08/IES-presentation-2-13xmhdj.pdf

Prins, E., & Gungor, R. (2011). Family literacy funding reductions and work-first welfare policies: Adaptations and consequences in family literacy programs. *Adult Basic Education and Literacy Journal, 5*(1), 15–25.

Prins, E., & Kassab, C. (2015). GED recipients in postsecondary education: A rural-urban analysis of Pennsylvania FAFSA applicants' educational, demographic, and financial characteristics. *Journal of Research and Practice for Adult Literacy, Secondary, and Basic Education, 4*(2), 20–36.

Prins, E., Kassab, C., Drayton, B., & Gungor, R. (2012). Distance learning for GED students in rural Pennsylvania. *American Journal of Distance Education, 26*(4), 217–235.

Prins, E., & Toso, B. W. (2012). Receptivity toward immigrants in rural Pennsylvania: Perceptions of adult English as second language providers. *Rural Sociology, 77*(3), 435–461.

Rank, M. R. (2004). *One nation, underprivileged: Why American poverty affects us all.* Oxford: Oxford University Press.

Smith, M. W., Appleman, D., & Wilhelm, J. D. (2014). *Uncommon core: Where the authors of the standards go wrong about instruction-and how you can get it right.* Thousand Oaks, CA: Corwin Press.

Thiede, B., Greiman, L., Weiler, S., Beda, S. C., & Conroy, T. (2017). Six charts that illustrate the divide between rural and urban America. Retrieved from https://theconversation.com/six-charts-that-illustrate-the-divide-between-rural-and-urban-america-72934

U.S. Department of Agriculture Economic Research Service. (2015). *Rural America at a glance, 2015 edition.* Retrieved from https://www.ers.usda.gov/webdocs/publications/44015/55581_eib145.pdf?v=42397

DR. ESTHER PRINS *is a professor in the Lifelong Learning and Adult Education Program at Penn State and the co-director of the Goodling Institute for Research in Family Literacy and the Institute for the Study of Adult Literacy.*

INDEX

National Reporting System (NRS), 14, 20, 62
National Research Council (NRC), 85, 90
National Workforce Demonstration Projects, 12
Needle, M., 100
Neff, D., 86
Ness, M., 97
Network literacy, 54
New Literacy Studies (NLS), 98
Newman, A., 51
No Child Left Behind Act, 79
Noguerón-Liu, S., 53
Noss, R., 86
Numeracy and mathematics research, 86–88

O'Donoghue, J., 86
Office of Career, Technical, and Adult Education (OCTAE), 24, 54
Office of Vocational and Adult Education (OVAE), 11, 75
Organisation for Economic Cooperation and Development's (OECD), 6, 30, 52
Oughton, H., 87, 88

Pae, H., 84
Pahl, K., 98
Palm, T., 87
Park, M., 89
Passel, J. S., 64
Patterson, M. B., 85
Payne, E. M., 78
Pearson VUE computer labs, 45
Pegrum, M., 54
Pennsylvania Association for Adult Education, 96
Personal Responsibility and Work Opportunity Act, 20
Pete, J. K., 66
Peters, S. J., 101
Pickard, A., 25, 57
Pimentel, S., 22, 42, 55, 97, 98
Pitkin, J., 67
Porter, K. E., 85
Prewett, S., 85
Price, L., 57
Prins, E., 95, 96, 98, 100, 103
Problem Solving in Technology Rich Environments (PS-TRE), 30, 35, 52
Professionalization, defined, 76

Program for International Assessment of Adult Competence (PIAAC), 6, 29–30, 52; data to support investment, 37–38; DeSeCo, 30–33; guide instruction, 33–37
Program for International Student Assessment (PISA), 31

Rank, M. R., 100
Raymond, B., 100
Reardon, R. F., 78
Reder, S., 52, 57, 85
Redman, R., 56
Research, reading, 83–85
Reumann, R., 101
Richer, E., 90
Rosbash, T., 51
Rose, A., 20
Rose, A. D., 11
Rosen, D., 57
Rosen, D. J., 51, 60
Rosin, M., 77
Rowe, K., 72, 73
Rumbaut, R. G., 61
Russell, M., 77
Rychen, D. S., 30, 31
Rytina, N., 63, 64

Sabatini, J., 83, 84
Sabatini, J. P., 77, 84
Salganik, L. H., 30, 31
Samuels, S., 84
Santos, F., 96
Sarkisian, L., 51
Sawaki, Y., 83, 84
Scarborough, H., 83, 84
Shanahan, T., 76
Shore, J., 83, 84
Shrestha, S., 67
Sitomer, A., 87
Smith, C., 23, 71, 72, 73, 76, 77, 81
Smith, M.W., 97
Smith, N., 42
Solomon, M., 72, 73
Spence, R., 90
State and Local Workforce Development Boards, 20
State Literacy Resource Centers (SLRC), 12
St. Clair, R., 12, 14
Stein, S. G., 29, 40

Practical facilitation techniques tailored to the adult brain

Facilitating Learning with the Adult Brain in Mind explains how the brain works and how to help adults learn, develop, and perform more effectively in various settings. Recent neurobiological discoveries have challenged long-held assumptions that logical, rational thought is the preeminent approach to knowing. Rather, feelings and emotions are essential for meaningful learning to occur in the embodied brain. Using stories, metaphors, and engaging illustrations to illuminate technical ideas, Taylor and Marienau synthesize relevant trends in neuroscience, cognitive science, and philosophy of mind.

This book provides facilitators of adult learning and development a much-needed resource of tested approaches plus the science behind their effectiveness.

- Appreciate the fundamental role of experience in adult learning

- Understand how metaphor and analogy spark curiosity and creativity

- Alleviate adult anxieties that impede learning

- Acquire tools and approaches that foster adult learning and development

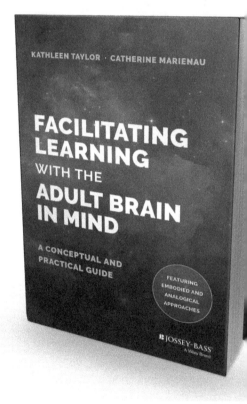

KATHLEEN TAYLOR · CATHERINE MARIENAU

FACILITATING LEARNING WITH THE **ADULT BRAIN IN MIND**

A CONCEPTUAL AND PRACTICAL GUIDE

FEATURING EMBODIED AND ANALOGICAL APPROACHES

JB JOSSEY-BASS
A Wiley Brand

 **Also available as an e-book.**

NEW DIRECTIONS FOR ADULT AND CONTINUING EDUCATION

ORDER FORM SUBSCRIPTION AND SINGLE ISSUES

DISCOUNTED BACK ISSUES:

Use this form to receive 20% off all back issues of *New Directions for Adult and Continuing Education*.
All single issues priced at **$23.20** (normally $29.00)

TITLE	ISSUE NO.	ISBN

Call 1-800-835-6770 or see mailing instructions below. When calling, mention the promotional code JBNND to receive your discount. For a complete list of issues, please visit www.wiley.com/WileyCDA/WileyTitle/productCd-ACE.html

SUBSCRIPTIONS: (1 YEAR, 4 ISSUES)

☐ New Order   ☐ Renewal

U.S.	☐ Individual: $89	☐ Institutional: $356
CANADA/MEXICO	☐ Individual: $89	☐ Institutional: $398
ALL OTHERS	☐ Individual: $113	☐ Institutional: $434

Call 1-800-835-6770 or see mailing and pricing instructions below.
Online subscriptions are available at www.onlinelibrary.wiley.com

ORDER TOTALS:

Issue / Subscription Amount: $ _____

Shipping Amount: $ _____
(for single issues only – subscription prices include shipping)

Total Amount: $ _____

SHIPPING CHARGES:	
First Item	$6.00
Each Add'l Item	$2.00

(No sales tax for U.S. subscriptions. Canadian residents, add GST for subscription orders. Individual rate subscriptions must be paid by personal check or credit card. Individual rate subscriptions may not be resold as library copies.)

BILLING & SHIPPING INFORMATION:

☐ **PAYMENT ENCLOSED:** *(U.S. check or money order only. All payments must be in U.S. dollars.)*

☐ **CREDIT CARD:** ☐ VISA ☐ MC ☐ AMEX

Card number _____ Exp. Date _____

Card Holder Name_____ Card Issue # _____

Signature _____ Day Phone _____

☐ **BILL ME:** *(U.S. institutional orders only. Purchase order required.)*

Purchase order # _____
Federal Tax ID 13559302 • GST 89102-8052

Name _____

Address_____

Phone_____ E-mail_____

Copy or detach page and send to: **John Wiley & Sons, Inc. / Jossey Bass**
PO Box 55381
Boston, MA 02205-9850

PROMO JBNND